ADVENTURES
IN CHILD'S PLAY

*A history of children's
play provision in the UK*

RAY WILLS

DEDICATION

This book is dedicated to the late W D (DRUMMOND) ABERNETHY (1913–1988). Former teacher, who worked for the Educational division of the Rank organisation until he joined (N.P.F.A) National Playing Fields

Drummond W.D Abernethy

Association from 1956–1977 and became head of their Children's Play Department. He was also a member of numerous national and governmental youth organisations and Secretary to the International Playground Association (1963–1972).

Without his tireless work dedication, support and encouragement I would not have been involved in the field of Children's Play. Drummond inspired me from the start in the very early days with his eloquent speeches his advice and knowledge. From the time when I first heard of the National Playing Fields (now Fields In Trust) and was trained under his watchful eye at Playfield House London in the mid 1960s and throughout my career until his death in the 1980s. Without his input Child's Play would not have developed and been such a major success in so many parts of the UK, Europe and abroad. If Lady Allen is regarded by many as the God Mother of Play then Drummond surely was Child's Plays own God Father.

TABLE OF CONTENTS

SUMMARY

ACKNOWLEDGEMENTS

SOURCES RESOURCES AND RECCOMENDED
READINGS

PREFACE FOREWORD

FOREWORD

ADVENTURES IN CHILDS PLAY is written by Ray Wills an accomplished children's play organiser with very many years of experience of play provision in the UK. Ray writes a very personal account about those early years of children's play provision in the UK much of it based on his own experiences. He writes of a time when child's play was in its infancy. From the days when children were playing on bombed wastelands of the cities, the junk playgrounds of the post war years to the modern day supervised adventure playgrounds and play facilities. The book is packed with stories and Rays recollections of those years with details of the people, places and events which shaped the future of play. Along with the numerous campaigns which led to the growth and establishment of play provision in the UK as the child's right. It includes detailed histories and accounts of numerous adventure playgrounds, play centres and schemes which operated throughout the UK. Many of which are based on Rays own recollections and his own personal involvement at the time. This book is an essential source and asset for all those who work in or are in some way involved in the field of children's play. As well as those who work with children daily, such as teachers and students of social science and social psychology. This new publication includes art illustrations and photographs.

ABOUT THE AUTHOR

Raymond Wills

Ray Wills is no newcomer to the field of Children's Play provision having spent many decades working in the UK promoting establishing and operating a vast variety of adventure playgrounds, play centres and town wide play schemes. Ray is also an accomplished author and poet. His previous publications have included handbooks on play for the National Playing Fields Association and editing of an anthology of stories and poetry entitled GYPSY STORYTELLERS published by Francis Boutle Publishers. Ray was involved in the early development of Adventure Playgrounds and the formation of numerous play forums, councils and play steering committees when Child's play was still in its infancy. A former Fellow member of the Institute of Play and The National Association of Recreation Leaders. Ray has years of experience in all areas of community work including the formation of action groups, tenant/resident bodies and pressure groups. He is qualified in both Youth Work -(City and Guilds) and Community Project management- Dip Mgt-(Royal Society of Arts).

INTRODUCTION

"If you are going to keep children safe you must provide trees they can climb and ways in which they can safely get the experience of adventure and the sense of challenge that they crave".-ISSACS

"To climb a new tree is to discover a new world, seen from above everything looks different from the usual telescoped distorted side view. If we could remember our joy when in childhood we looked out beyond the crampling limit of our immediate surroundings we should not be a insensitive to call out, Come down you will fall".-FROBEL

"That every child has the right to rest and leisure, to engage in play and recreational activities appropriate to the age of the child and to participate freely in cultural life and the arts"."That member governments shall respect and promote the right of the child to participate fully in cultural and artistic life and shall encourage the provision of appropriate and equal opportunities for cultural, artistic, recreational and leisure activity."

Article 31 of the UN Convention

"The history of childhood is a nightmare from which we have only recently begun to awaken"- Lloyd Demause.

"At first they dug in the earth and used builder's bricks to construct their houses, but after they had got experience in handling tools and material, they made many complicated projects, and at the end of six months, the "Waste material playground" was made"- Emdrupt .

Where as a kid I played

I remember the quarry's and the little shaded nook

the meadows where we built our dens next to the little brook

the trees that soared up to the skies where birds hid and built
their nests

the hidden place behind the church where no one ever
looked

Each summertime on Wareham's walls where lizards all did
squirm

amongst the adder and the ferns where the shiny fat slow
worms

all hid themselves from man and beast wherein the kids did
play

close by the river Frame and Stour as if it was yesterday

The Canford walks with sandy lanes and gorse bush
spreading free

where gypsy man and gypsy tan mixed so heavenly

the hills and dips where robbers hid and cowboys played at
dawn

where robins sang and everyone was happy in their place

I remember it like yesterday as Johnny onion came to call

with bicycles laden rich with giant dangling onion balls

the streets were narrow and the hedges graced the fields

where sparrows chirped each day at dawn and flew off
window sills

The lights were dim and green so blessed with ironmongery
rich

whilst sailors sailed from old Poole quay and gals they took
a hitch

the rabbits ran across the downs and guns were fired at dawn

whilst farmers chased the foxes and the daisies graced the
lawns

I remember summers long and winter snow was thick

we hid upon the bracken then close by the little ditch

our dens were neat and tidy with straw and mattress thick

we ran the hills and downs of land that man took and sold
off for rich

I recall the ins and outs the little shop nearby

where sherbet dibs were squandered for some gals pleasant
eye

the running brooks and meadows sweet with rhododendrons
nearby

it vanished in a moment as all the years went bye

Ray Wills

*"In play, a child is always above his average age, above his daily
behaviour; in play, it is as though he were a head taller than
himself."*- Lev Vygotsky (1896-1934)

There have been numerous studies of children's play throughout
the years from social historians, psychologists and so called play
experts of all kinds. Most of them analytical or theoretical, with
some based on actual day to day work with children such as play
workers or adventure playground workers. I hope this book is
much different and fulfils my hope as there is so much theory out
there and not enough down to earth involvement and real life
stories. I believe this book in many ways will fulfil that need for
a real life look into the child's world of play.

When a child has lost the ability to play, he is psychically dead
and a danger to any child who comes into contact with him. —
A. S. Neill.

Ray Wills a child on the Mannings Heath.

The play of children has always held a special fascination for me. With my own childhood play experiences being so full, I guess in many ways this was inevitable. I was raised by my grand-parents at the family small holding farm (The Manning's), on Lady Wimborne Estate at Canford Heath, Poole, Dorset. Throughout our childhood we took risks we learnt what our capabilities were and to stretch ourselves. To always tried new things and many fresh challenges, whether swinging from a high Tarzan rope then jumping off onto a far bank or onto a sandy or grassy surface. We climbed trees, balanced, ourselves on branches stepping from one to another or swinging down to earth. We learnt to use balance, we stepped across streams and rivers on rocks and stones. We lit fires made from furze, brushwood and gathered together around them or built larger bonfires from driftwood on the sandy or chisel stone beaches. Sitting around these lit fires and watching the sparks and embers.

Here we talked for hours enjoying this pleasure associated with the open fire an experience which few children experience today. Each year on November 5th we lit large bonfires celebrating Guy Fawkes day, firetens which took us weeks to build as a team of kids. We learnt what the dangers were from our first hand experience, we jumped or dived off of stone bridges into rivers far below. We used tools and gathered whatever waste materials were at hand to build our hideouts and dens in the woods or any available wastelands. We were adventurous, challenging, free spirited and happy in our play work. Children built underground dens in the sandy mounds on the heath, these ingenious underground dens were all padded out on the inside, with mattresses and carpets. Then covered over the top with a roof made of tin sheeting at ground level. Then cleverly covered over with sods of grass; as camouflage, all well hidden from adult prying eyes. Trees would be conquered and used for rope Tarzan swings, with their high branches to hang from; using disgraced or abandoned car tires, or a stick as the seat. Such swings when in use rotated in large circular movements with a high drop below, with us children falling safely onto sandy surfaces. This was often to be our only escape in a moment of danger.

Close to my childhood home there was a large abandoned red sandy quarry with a reservoir nearby, often used by hordes of us children for playing games and adventurous pursuits. It was here where we built special camps and dens similar to caves, into the sides of the quarries sandy red banks. We would often swim naked in the wide, but safe pool of water, which in actual fact was a reservoir. Such places were our own personal adventure playgrounds. There was little housing then, no roads for miles and with only bird song, gypsy caravans and sand lizards for company a great deal of the time. Despite all this our childhood play world then was a great deal safer then than the present 21st Century environment. With its dangerous highways, heavy traffic, and crime, including that of the over played fear of "stranger's danger". Then children were able to roam for miles in complete safety, parents were not so concerned then as now. Though we were constantly warned of hidden dangers, such as a store of hidden ammunition, abandoned on the boggy heath left *over from the war years, containing grenades and mines embedded in the heath land mossy blanket. As a small boy, I was fascinated with the power of matches, on one occasion I caught fire to furze bushes on the common, which terrified me. I was unable to put the fire out, for it was spreading so quickly. Being midsummer, the day was very hot, however eventually three fire engines arrived. I was kept in my room and scolded for this major misdemeanour. Because of this frightening experience, I was determined in later years to work with others to provide safe play opportunities for children. To both control fires and to enjoy the excitement, energy and warmth of fires within supervised adventure playground environments. The many play opportunities provided to build, create and take responsibility for oneself was always a part of my childhood. My family taught me the basic skills involved in the building of chicken pens and bird aviaries, cow sheds and pig sties. Building skills which would all come in useful in later years, when I was to establish, operate and build Adventure Playgrounds. We would visit the local dump just across the heath, where we would explore the large amounts of timber cuts and other materials; which local companies dumped there and which we could freely use in our junk play.*

At the age of ten I moved to Wareham Dorset, a country holiday town, in the heart of the Purbeck Hills. Home of Thomas Hardy and William Barnes. Here I spent my play times with country farm children, exploring this most enchanting market town with its high undulating grassy banks of earthen grass walls, surrounding the town itself. It was here where I quickly grasped from other children, new skills, how to catch lizards on the high grass walls surrounding the town, or fish for minnows from the rivers. We kids built strong earthen forts and wooden dens on the wasteland opposite the Church of Lady St. Mary's. Here we had our own community for one long hot summer. Other times we would go paddling at the sandy white sandpits, close to the mill where the mad miller of Wareham town once lived. During the long summer months and school holidays, many kids would build wooden Go-karts, constructed from fruit boxes and pram wheels and ride them around the grass pathways and slopes of the walls, which encircled the town. The town itself was particularly safe for a vast variety of more adventurous activities, for there were few dangerous side roads at that time and it was very child friendly. In my youth living at nearby Bovington, I spent summer holidays in the woodlands with others, building hide outs, using discarded pigs sties houses of galvanised sheeting, stuffed with straw begged from the local military stables. Taking part in large gatherings of our peers at organised barbecues on the local beaches at Durdle Door and Lulworth Cove. Collecting large pieces of driftwood washed ashore from the sea, to make large bonfires on the sandy or rocky beaches close to cave entrances. Gathering in large numbers of youths from around the Dorset county, playing guitars, singing folk songs and drinking draught cider previously rolled down the cliffs in large barrels.

I Remember

I Remember, I Remember,
The House Where I Was Born,
The Little Window Where The Sun
Came Peeping Through At Dawn,
He Never Came A Wink Too Soon,
Nor Bright Too Long A Day,
But Now I Often Wish The Night
Had Borne My Breath Away.
I Remember, I Remember,
The Roses, Red And White,
The Violets And The Lily Cups -
Those Flowers Made Of Light
The Lilacs Where The Robin Built,
And Where My Brother Set
The Laburnum On His Birthday -
The Tree Is Living Yet.
I Remember, I Remember
Where I Was Used To Swing,
And Thought The Air Must Rush As Fresh
To Swallows On The Wing
My Spirit Flew In Feathers Then
That Is So Heavy Now,
The Summer Pools Could Hardly Cool

The Fever On My Brow.
I Remember, I Remember,
The Fir Trees Dark And High,
I Used To Think Their Slender Tops,
Were Close Against The Sky.
It Was A Childish Ignorance,
But Now 'Tis Little Joy,
To Know I'm Further Off From Heaven,
Then When I Was A Boy.

-Thomas Hood (The Plea Of The Midsummer Fairies 1827)

When I left school my first jobs in Dorset were as painter and decorator at Bluebirds Caravans Poole, a civilian officers Batman at Bovington Camp Officers Mess in Wareham and then store man positions. I joined (CSV) Community Service Volunteers at 21 after reading an article in the Sunday Pictorial encouraging young people to work on community service projects. Others entered the play work profession from a similar range of backgrounds, including Jim Jackson, who also came into play from (CSV) Community Service Volunteers. Whilst the original leader of Notting Hill Adventure Playground Pat Smyth was a former paratrooper. I have worked alongside other play people throughout the U.K, promoting and establishing a variety of play facilities for children of all ages. Such as adventure playgrounds, play centre's and play schemes. This is my account of those years and covers a period when Child's play provision was in its infancy with organizations like the (NPFA) National Playing Fields Association (Fields In Trust) playing a major role. My story includes the birth and establishment of a variety of pressure groups such as "Fair Play For Children" ,The Lollipop Brigade", "The Adventure Playground Workers Association" and "Safety on Playgrounds" initiatives. I was fortunate to work alongside many pioneers of play provision who were also my friends as well as recognized experts, members of parliament, national celebrities and the early pioneers, who all played their part in establishing Child's play as a right for all children. Often these were very small tiny children, only toddlers just learning to walk whilst other small or older children were often busy occupied in boisterous excited games or in imaginative and creative activities. Each one working in their particular play occupations for play was their work, here they were constantly creating and using their creative imaginations and physical energies within a free community setting of peers of all ages and abilities. I was with others of like minds over the years employed by both local authorities and voluntary community groups as the Child's enablers or play leaders/play workers. From the early 1950s we worked in a variety of settings throughout the U.K some of these were in inner city urban, multi cultural/racial and socially deprived areas. Others in the emerging new towns, or on large housing estates or in remote villages. Through these changing years I worked alongside many of these pioneers and ambassadors of play. As well as advocates of both play bodies and recognized national organizations which were emerging after the war years. This is my story of those years and the people who helped to shape and to make Child's play provision in the UK become a reality. People like Drummond Abernethy, Lady Marjorie Allen, Marie Paneth, Tony Chilton, Jack Lambert, Donne Buck and Joe Benjamin. These in particular made a lasting impression amongst many others who are too numerous to mention. To which we owe a great debt of gratitude.

CHAPTER ONE

THE FORMATIVE YEARS OF PLAY PROVISION IN THE UK

"To desire to experiment and to build, to find out for himself, it is natural and necessary to the twelve year old, as to the sand and water stage to the three year olds; The adventure playground was conceived specifically for this, to provide for this kind of activity, it was to be the workshop of the child"- -Joe Benjamin / Leader of London Adventure Playground.

" It is like putting a magnifying glass on the community"-Francis McLennan / Leader of Angel Town Adventure Playground-London.

"Adventure playgrounds are places where children of all ages can develop their own ideas of play. Most young people, at one time or another, have a deep urge to experiment with earth, fire, water and timber, to work with real tools without fear of undue

1

criticism or censure. In these playgrounds their love of freedom to take calculated risks is recognized and can be enjoyed under tolerant and sympathetic guidance." -Lady Marjorie Allen

Lollard st adventure playground

A Good Play

We built a ship upon the stairs
All made of the back room chairs
And filled it full of soft pillows

We took a saw and several nails
And water in the nursery pails
And Tom said Let us also take an apple and a slice of cake
Which was enough for You and Me
To go a sailing on till tea

We sailed for days and days
And had the very best of plays
But Tom fell out and hurt his knee

So there was no one left but me..

Robert Louis Stevenson1885.

There was a child went forth every day, And the first object he looked upon and received with wonder, pity, love, or dread, that object he became, And that object became part of him for the day, or a certain part of day, or for many years, or stretching cycles of years.
                                        —Walt Whitman, Leaves of Grass, 1856

"City streets are unsatisfactory playgrounds for children because of the danger, because most good games are against the law, because they are too hot in summer, and because in crowded sections of the city they are apt to be schools of crime. Neither do small back yards nor ornamental grass plots meet the needs of any but the very small children ... since play is a fundamental need, playgrounds should be provided for every child as much as schools".1907 President Theodore Roosevelt

The history of the child play movement in the U.K is short. For generations children play was condemned by adults as an intrusion into their Adult world of work and leisure. Up until the 19th Century, once a small child had grown out of the nappy stage and could walk, the child was expected to play an active role in family life. Childhood as a vocation, was not recognised as having any value, special attention or provision. "In 1385, the Bishop of London complained of children playing around St. Paul's and in 1447 the Bishop of Exeter also complained of children playing within the church cloisters during services. An Italian visitor to England remarked in his 'Revelations' of the late 15th Century "The want of affection in the English, is directly manifested towards their children. For often having kept them at home till they arrive at the age of 7 or 8 years, or 9 at the utmost, they put them out to hard service in the houses of other people, binding them for another 7 or 9 years". In London, a Beadle was employed to whip children away from the Royal exchange.

It is only in recent times that child's play was to eventually become excepted and seen as being of any real value or worth in society. For it wasn't until the 1800s that even the period we know today as childhood was to be given any recognition and became accepted. There were moves by a few radical thinkers to provide provision for children such as Robert Owen who in 1810 was operating special day nurseries for infants at his New Lanark mills, where three and four year old s danced and sang together. Whilst church groups and others such as the Children's Holiday Fund and The Fresh Air Fund, Band of Hope and Salvation Army operated a range of activities for children. By 1848 all local council authorities in the UK had statutory powers to provide for the means of education or amusement to the middle or humbler classes. Though the *century had heralded in new children's rights, reforms and social recreations and was heralded* by historians as, " The Century of the Child".44 Soon there were play areas playgrounds established in many cities such as at *Queens Park in Manchester and Barbary street in Birmingham. These contained swings, ball and shuttle cock areas, archery area, skipping area, swings grounds and a cricket ground, though these were all private.*

It was the teacher, writer and visionary William Barnes of Dorchester (Dorset) who had first saw the threat to the play of children, with the decline of natural play places. In his visionary poem entitled The Lane.

The Lane.
They do say that a travelling chap
have a put in the newspapers now,
that the bit of grass ground on the knap
should all be taken for the plough.
He do fancy that it is easy to show
that we can be but stupid at best,
for to leave a green spot where a flower can grow
or a foot weary walker can rest.

It's hedge grabbing, Thomas, and ledge-grabbing
never a done while a sovereign mores to be gained.
Years ago the lane's sides did bear grass
for to pull with the geese red bills,
that did hiss at the folks that did pass,
or the boys that picked up their white quills.

But soon if flower or life of
our goslings do creep from the egg,
they must mope in the garden, more dead than alive
in a coop or else tied by their leg,
for to catch at the land, Thomas, and snatch at land,
now is the plan - Make money wherever you can.

For to breed the young fox or the hare
we can give up whole acres of ground,
but the greens be a grudged, for to rear
our young children up healthy and strong,
why, there won't be left in the next age
a green spot where their feet can run free,
and the cuckoo will soon be committed to cage
for trespassing in somebody's tree,
for it's locking up, Thomas,
and blocking up stranger or brother
- Men mustn't come near one another

~by William Barnes
(translated into national English by Raymond Wills)

There were many radical welfare changes in the emerging 20th
century. By 1907 with the establishment of separate juvenile
court system their first probation officers were all recruited from
play centre workers. Robert Baden-Powell had founded the
Scouts Association first camp on Brownsea Island (Poole in

Dorset). Whilst nearby at Shaftesbury (Dorset) Homer Lane had established the first free school "The Little Commonwealth' in 1913. Homer Lane commentated -"the child in the playground was not the same child who came to school, resourceful and purposeful, all qualities apparent in his spontaneous play" (This influenced Coldwell Cooks book 'The Free Way' published in 1917). The McMillan sisters (Margaret and Rachel) who came from the states founded the "Open Air Movement" which established one of England's first school-based health clinics. Margaret McMillan beliefs were that children should have regular access to the outdoors to assist their development. "By giving children physical development it helps stimulate the child, and helps the children develop their five senses as they are touching grass, smelling the air , seeing flowers grow, hearing birds and insects and tasting fruit that is growing outside in their environment". The early exponents of Play felt that a lack of opportunity for healthy spontaneous play activities may well be responsible for much defective bodily development. For Play brought the child into the open air, it gives him a better body and improves his nutrition and makes him more resistant to disease. Another pioneer was Mary Ward one of the founders of the settlement movement and her involvement led to play centre's being introduced for the first time for children of working mothers and by 1915 22 of these play centre's were operational whilst others like The "Children's Happy Evenings Association" also had nearly 100 play centre's in operation. Dame Grace Mary Thyrza Kimmins, was the driving force behind the "Guild of Play" and 6 of these were established in Croydon London and other cities throughout the UK. Eglantyne Jebb and her sister Dorothy Buxton campaigned and set up "The Save the Children Fund" at a public meeting in London's Royal Albert Hall in May of 1919. Charles Wicksteed established his company manufacturing unsupervised play equipment at Kettering: These were popular with both children and Adults. Wicksteed remarked - "I have seen a dozen women of forty on the jazzy plank swings and enjoying it as much as the children". "I have also seen old ladies of eighty go on the slides".

"ALL DRESSED UP BUT NOWHERE TO GO"

KEEP OFF THE GRASS

Help the
National Playing Fields
Association

Then in 1925 The National Playing Fields Association was founded when Murray Lawes a close friend of Wykeham Stanley Cornwallis knew the Brigadier-General Reginald Kentish. They helped set up the (NPFA) National Playing Fields Association through the Royal Charter. The objective being to acquire, protect and improve playing fields, playgrounds and play areas where they were most needed, and for those who most needed them. A very big meeting was held in the Royal Albert Hall, London, to launch the National Playing Fields Association, and the King who was the then Duke of York became its first President. Lloyd George in a message to the National Playing Fields Association at that time said:" The right to play is a child's first claim on the community. No community can infringe that right without doing deep and enduring harm to the minds and bodies of its citizens". At that time and throughout the 1930s the Carnegie UK Trust gave grants of over £200,000 to the (NPFA) National Playing Fields Association to help establish 900 playing fields across the UK and Ireland. (But no central record of these fields were kept). The (NPFA) National Playing Fields Association set itself the task of providing enough playing fields for all sections of the community and well-equipped playgrounds for children and later of encouraging the training of Play Leaders. In those early days they also subsidized train and bus fares so that children were able to facilitate playing fields and gave grant aid to set up the Central Council of Physical Recreation. At that time play parks were also established throughout the country under the Government campaign "A Fitter Britain Movement". Lady Marjorie Allen of Hurtwood was involved in their development as chair of the Coronation planting committee. Prior to the 1939-1945 war the (N.P.F.A) National Playing Fields Association were displaying posters showing city children pathetically trying to amuse themselves in dangerous crowded streets because there was nowhere else for them to play. It had raised money mainly by public subscription, whilst maintaining a service of technical and practical advice to local authorities, clubs and other voluntary bodies. Over the years since its formation the (N.P.F. A) National Playing Fields Association had raised their funds from various sources. Including "The Variety Club of Great Britain" at their annual awards and dinners, "The Gold Diggers" with their celebrities charity soccer matches and through the very popular Billy Butlins holiday camps. Numerous Pathe news films were also made involving stars of stage and screen such as Bob Hope, Kenneth Moore, Kathleen Harrison, Wilfred Pickles, Ronald Shiner etc. Which brought the matter of the need for spaces for Child's play, to the general public attention. As well as raising much needed donations towards playing fields and playgrounds. Top recording stars such as Sinatra and Elton John made records providing royalties to the funds of (NPFA)The National Playing Fields Association. As well as famous soccer stars such as Jimmy Hill, both Elton and Jimmy who were regular visitors to (NPFAs) National Playing Fields Association Playfield House on numerous occasions , as well as its President HRH Prince Philip the Duke of Edinburgh. In its history up to the mid 1980s the N.P.F.A had invested more than £2 million in acquiring, developing, improving and developing recreational facilities.

Adventure Junk Playground Origins

The history of the adventure playground and the free play work movement, has its roots as early as 1931 when the Danish Architect . Sorenson had a dream which he published in "Park Politics in Town and Country". In which he coined the phrase 'Junk Playground' which was based on his observations of children playing on empty building sites. Mr. Sorensen, who had laid out many orthodox playgrounds had observed that children seemed to get more pleasure when they trespassed into the building sites and played with the materials they found there. The children appeared excited by the endless possibilities that these construction site offered them in creating their own adventures. He decided to integrate this idea into the designs for the open spaces he and his colleagues were designing for the new Danish housing associations and parks. Sorenson stated "Finally we should probably at some point experiment with what one could call a junk playground". "I am thinking in terms of an area, not too small in size, well closed off from its surroundings by thick greenery, where we should gather, for the amusement of bigger children, all sorts of old scrap that the children from the apartment blocks could be allowed to work with, as the children in the countryside and in the suburbs already have". "That perhaps we should set up waste material playgrounds in suitable large areas, where children could play with old cars, boxes and timber". "Of course some kind of order would have to be maintained; but I believe that things would not need to go radically wrong with that sort of situation". "If there were really a lot of space, one is tempted to imagine tiny little kindergartens, keeping hens and the like, but it would at all events require an interested adult supervisor".

One of the very first attempts to provide community based organized activities in the UK for the whole family. Prior to the war years including that of play provision had been "The Peckham Experiment". This project operated in London from 1935 right up to the outbreak of the second world war in 1939. Play streets and Belisha beacons were introduced in 1935 by Leslie Hore-Belisha and The Street Playgrounds Act later in 1938.This allowed local authorities to close residential streets to traffic between 8am and sunset in concern about the number of children being killed or injured in road accidents. During 1938 Lady Marjorie Allen had delivered a paper entitled "The Future of Landscape Architecture" in which she described a Welsh park where children were permitted to both dig and to dwell. She posed it as The ideal playground as it made the children "blissfully happy".

During the war years of 1939-1945 many children had taken part in a variety of play schemes on the London undergrounds and in the air raid shelters during the bombings. These were often the only safe places for families sheltering from the constant bombing. Children's misbehaviour had become a major problem in these air raid shelters and evacuation centres, where the children were seen as too disruptive and rough to be evacuated with other city children. As a result the government was compelled to introduce play centres as a way to keep the children happy. Marie Paneth an Austrian Artist, teacher and writer was commissioned to work with them. Paneth had originally visited the Tilbury Shelter in the East End for the purpose of studying at first hand the conditions under which family life continued during the blitz. Branch Street was based on Clarendon Crescent Tilbury in Paddington, very close to Little Venice an area where few settled. It was a project which had originated from the work of a group of volunteers concerned at the wildness and poverty of the children who gathered in the air raid shelters. She started work in her Branch Street project in Paddington in 1940 setting up her play centre initially in an air raid shelter then later at a condemned house in a street close to a bomb shelter. The scheme operated till 1942. The house had been handed over to her by the local borough council. More than 100 children lived in the Branch street where there was a great deal of poverty, poor health and many family breakdowns. All of Marie's early play centres were staffed mainly by conscientious objectors, Quakers and pacifists. Marie was influenced by the ideas of August Aitchhan an Austrian social worker and encouraged by the earlier success of Ruth and David Wills at Barns House in Scotland in 1937. Where David and Ruth Wills had worked with between 50 to 60 maladjusted boys who were evacuees from Edinburgh. Branch street was a place where children gained the attention of friendly Adults supervision and Marie concentrated on the use of therapeutic art to assist these boisterous wild children who had suffered such traumatic experiences. She believed that such play opportunities were the answer to resolve their undisciplined ways of thieving and violence and which allowed them to deal with all their traumas and to master them. She was of the opinion that playing could have a healing effect if they were allowed to create upon the very spot where so much damage had been done. Paneth advocated working with these disruptive and troubled kids on a specially designed playground/bomb site. She deliberately choose to work with such "Hooligans" and had a strong belief in trying to work in a way that encouraged the children to take responsibility and to organize things for themselves. These children were brought up to expect that everyone will hate and despise them and so behaved accordingly. They were very unpleasant to her at times and she was not optimistic about their future. Marie commented "Once I spoke to them and tried to explain that everything used in the Play Centre belonged to them; was brought for their own use. If they broke things or destroyed them, they spoiled their own belongings and, if they took them away, their own things disappeared and they could not use them any more. This seemed to make a certain impression on them as a new thought, but it did not stop them from breaking and destroying."If we tried to impose control, we'd have a smaller but much nicer group, but would not be working with those who need us most."During her time with these children she discovered that the best way to control their boisterous and violent behaviour was to stop trying to control it. She provided them with their own Junk playground filled with broken and waste resources that they could identify with and focus on. In this way they learnt to work together as a group and worked out their aggression until they "became sick of their own method and could start life at the new place with rule and order." Here they created their own play spaces, secret playground where they lit illegal fires from wood stolen from bombed houses, and cooked stolen potatoes: "Now I came to them as somebody who tried to share what they did". "It was something very different from their coming to us, to the strange house and into a new situation". "Their attitude changed completely." The change in place altered the relationship she had with them, which worked to reduce their aggression. This development led Paneth to propose a new kind of play centre, in which children are provided with a bombed site, damaged like themselves, where they could build their own house with salvaged building materials. In many ways she was one of the very first advocates of adventure play in the UK and voiced her strong views that there should be supervised adventure playgrounds on the bombed sites. Paneth proposed providing these slum children with building materials to build a house for themselves. These were a blueprint for the future adventure playgrounds philosophy with their use of bombed sites and the self building philosophy.

Marie Paneth- "There is a bombed site quite near to Branch Street. It is a biggish place with even a few trees standing on it and lots of bricks lying about. I would like to see the children on this site busy building a hut or a house for themselves. If they could have the use of this place and one could find a man who not only understands the type of child but who knows how to lay bricks and can help them with the construction, they could be constructively busy in the healthiest way for many months". "They should be made the landlords. They should be the ones who are asked by the official to sign the document giving them the use of this bit of London for the duration. It seems to me it could have a very healing effect if one were allowed to build upon the very spot where damage has been done".- "Branch Street -A Sociological Study 1944".

George Orwell the author commenting on Paneths Branch Street- "Her book reveals the almost savage conditions in which some London children still grow up. It is not quite clear, however, whether these conditions are to any extent worse as a result of the war. I should like to read, I suppose some such thing must exist somewhere, but I don't know of it, an authoritative account of the effect of the war on children". Orwell described the children of Branch Street as "little better than savages". "They were not only dirty, ragged, under-nourished and unbelievably obscene in language and corrupt in outlook, but they were all thieves, and as intractable as wild animals. A few of the girls were approachable, but the boys simply smashed up the play centre over and over again, sometimes breaking in at night to do the job more thoroughly, and at times it was even dangerous for a grown-up to venture among them single-handed." "With such a background they have neither the chance of a worthwhile job nor, as a rule, the capacity for steady work. At best they find their way into some blind-alley occupation, but are more likely to end up in crime or prostitution," Gerge Orwell concludes: "'Branch Street' will go on creating wild and hopeless children until it has been abolished and rebuilt along with the other streets that have the same atmosphere". In other words, not enough had been done to clear the slums". " The children described by Mrs Paneth sound almost like the gangs of 'wild children' who were a by-product of the Russian Revolution".- George Orwell

Lady Marjorie Allen

Lady Marjorie Allen was undoubtedly the major figure in child welfare at that time as well as being involved in the organisation of "Operation Pied Piper" the evacuation of London children from the city to the country. Almost 2 million children were evacuated from the cities into the country areas; thanks in the main to the work of Herbert Morrisson Leader of the (LCC) London County Council. These children had to cope with rationing, gas masks lessons and living with complete strangers. (Children accounted for one in ten of the deaths during the Blitz of London). However many groups of youngsters were left behind, playing on the bombed sites of the city with schools closed. These children were unsupervised for most of the day as their fathers were away from home in the forces and their mothers were at work in the factories. These children were playing in somewhat undisciplined ways, yet within these groups yet there was often a discipline of sorts within the challenge of their building out of the risk and chaos.

A number of people at this period and earlier times had also been promoting the idea of Child's play in the open air including Susan Isaac's (1885-1948 and Margaret McMillan. Around that time a national advisory body was established alongside a government circular (no.1486) which saw their involvement in leisure time provision. So beginning the start of the partnership between the statutory authorities and the voluntary sector in leisure provision. At that time out of all young people between the ages of 14 to 20 years, only just one in eight were actually involved in any voluntary leisure activities.

Lady Marjorie Allen -The God Mother of Play.

At that time throughout Europe cities were devastated from the effects of the war, loss of lives and the constant bombings, with whole communities destroyed and left with just rubble and derelict land. Children had witnessed the loss of family members through the air raids or fighting in the war. All across Europe as a result of the bombing of the cities there were very many bombed wastelands and it was here children were playing. Using the materials readily available from bombed housing, such as bricks, timber, metal and any tools and equipment at hand to create their own junk playgrounds. Despite the warning signs on the sites children still played there totally ignoring all the apparent dangers just as if they never existed. Here they built their own clubhouses out of recycled timber with lino for roofing. In Britain throughout the war years and after and into the 1950s "youth" became a major problem to the British government. All of the cities at that time had become areas of bombed sites or houses left vacant and in rubble. But amongst this mess something extraordinary was happening. For many children these places held adventure and a means of creating good from bad. Here they played chase, sang their street rhymes or built impromptu dens out of discarded rubble, wood planking and tin sheeting. With a readily abundance of waste material at hand they created their dens and hideouts and to built and recreated out of the destruction that was all around them. Risks were plenty from the chance of discovering unexploded bombs or ammunition. Often more adventurous children climbing over half left dangerous buildings, brick rubble, glass windows, damaged doors etc and left over belongings from some ones former home. Children roamed in gangs throughout these wastelands and often they were very territorial with many clashes between children's gangs/ play communities to gain the spoils of war.

In 1942 Marjorie Allen pushed for the good quality timber from the wasteland bombed sites to be gathered by the defence workers. To be set aside for use by craftsmen from the Quakers community to construct toys and furniture for needy children and families.

Carl Theodor Sorensons dream became a reality -Emdrup The Junk playground

In 1943 in Emdrup Copenhagen Denmark a children's playground was developed under the watchful eyes of the German soldiers of occupation. Here children of all ages and abilities were encouraged by the Germans to create these playgrounds on the numerous bombed sites. The architect Dan Fink had commissioned Sorensen to design this junk playground as kind of children's republic. It was, fenced off from the outside world by a tall dyke; a 6ft. high bank with a thicket hedge and fence on top, which also absorbs the high frequencies of children's voices. Set in the "kingdom" of the Workers Co-operative Association housing estate just outside Copenhagen.

The Germans saw this as a way to deal with some of the problems they were encountering at the time with juvenile delinquency and anti social behaviour prevalent. Children were encouraged to create their very own junk playgrounds from out of the debris and rubble. Although Sorensen's initial idea was in fact a project without any Adult supervision however its first appointed play leader was John Bertelsen, a former Nursery Teacher and ex seaman . At the start as many as 900 children attended daily, soon levelling out to between 200 to 400 later. This junk playground was to become the child's workshop, providing a wide range and variety of building activities and creativeness. Bertelsen commented -"Then at last the company's carpenter arrived with the key, the door was opened and the children burst through completely taking over the playground, appropriating wheelbarrows and everything. The work was done by the children aged 4-17.It went on at full speed and all the work was in high spirits, dust sweat, warning shouts and a few scratches all created in just the right atmosphere. The children's play work ground had opened and they knew how to take full advantage of it". One observer noted " The children get three hundred building bricks and planks for the doors and roof". "These little houses are usually four feet by five feet but if many children work as a group, they can get six hundred bricks and make bigger houses with two or three rooms"."The bricks are cemented together with clay and made rainproof with grass". "The older children make fine houses with doors, complete with hinges and locks". "The girls decorate the houses inside and out,

17

put flowers in the windows, make tables, chairs and kitchen utensils". "Indian wigwams are made of laths of wood and branches of spruce in the shape of a bell-tent and some are twenty feet high".

During the initial three years and despite the numbers attending and the risky activities no serious accidents occurred. The reason being that the children were allowed to find out for themselves how far they can go with safety. The playground was n the main mostly visited by the so-called 'difficult' children and the children from large families and overcrowded homes. Initially intended for school age children, but, in reality its members were from infancy to eighteen years. Many children between the ages of five and fourteen, in order to play at all, had to chaperon their smaller brothers and sisters. Agnete Vesteregn, his ex-wife later replaced Bertelson in 1947.- Extracts - REAL PLAYGROUND - Picture Post 1946.

Sorenson remarked later that -;"The ugliest, yet for me it is the best and most beautiful of all my works". Yet the Emdrup play leader Bertelsen's predecessor, Vesteregn, who took over the

Emdrup playground later in 1947, rejected Bertelsen's permissive attitude toward lawlessness. Instead believing that "'children should not remain in [the] deconstructive state; they need help to be brought out of it".

Adventure play movement origins in the UK

London children playing amongst the bomb sites of the city

In the UK it was "The Under 14 Council" which was initially formed by Lady Allen, consisting of members from all the voluntary children's organisations met at (NPFA) s National Playing Fields Playfield House. (It operated until 1950 when it was merged as part of Save The Children Fund). A survey by Marjorie Allen's The "Under Fourteens Council" drew attention to the lack of play spaces in the UK, but also to the popularity of the bomb sites and the shells of half-destroyed houses. Marjorie Allen wrote a pamphlet for the Under14s Council in which she voiced her concerns.

Bomb sites were prevalent in practically all of the major cities of the UK and urban areas. These remained extremely popular with and amongst children who thronged to them in large numbers. Here their games were boisterous, challenging, unstructured creative and adventurous with a great deal of risk involved. There were serious concerns of what to do with these children who were now youths and the words juvenile delinquents ,teddy boys and juvenile gangs were in common use.

A good example portrayal of these times was in the 1947 Ealing Film comedy," Hue and Cry" starring young Harry Fowler, Jack Warner and a young Anthony Newley. Its story being based on the gangs of children frequenting and playing amongst the warren of London bomb sites with their secret societies. Here the children accepted bombed out London as their homeland and made their very own spaces amidst all of the rubble. The main gang of children who frequent the bomb sites in the Film were known as the "Blood and Thunder Boys". and were seen as a force to be reckoned with as they foiled the criminal gang.

During these days the local wardens chased children off of the bombed sites with all their dangers from unexploded bombs and debris. However these risks seemed to make such places more exciting and less of a deterrent to the majority of city children. The roads were gradually become no go areas for Child's play with the increased use of the motor car and the rise in road injuries. Such injuries and casualties was also becoming a serious problem for the government at that time. So that the development of play work and specifically adventure playgrounds were seen by many as being an answer by both dealing with the delinquency problem and the road safety concerns. As a result Government legislation was introduced by E.H. Keeting for the conversion of bombed sites into children's playgrounds. *Grant* aid had at last been made available for voluntary bodies working with children. Many solutions were put forward to deal with rising delinquency including that of play with leadership and some councils such as provided play activities in the parks. These first play park leaders were known as park Wardens and such schemes were operated in a variety of councils including Wandsworth and Peckham. The (N.P.F.A) National Playing Fields Association acted as an umbrella organization throughout England overseeing the development of all manner of children's play provision and encouraging other national bodies to set up a variety of similar schemes.

CHAPTER TWO

THE CHILDS WORKSHOP

Lollard Street adventure playground

"The right to play is a child's first claim on the community. Play is nature's training for life. No community can infringe that right without doing deep and enduring harm to the minds and bodies of its citizens" -David Lloyd George (1925).

"A good adventure playground is in a continual process of destruction and growth".- Lady Allen of Hurtwood.

Marjorie Allen campaigned through the Under 14 Council and as a result was called to give evidence of children made homeless or orphaned in Europe as a result of the war and particularly in the occupied nations. She was invited by the British Council to give a lecture tour in Norway. Consequently whilst embarking on journey on the 4th of March 1946 travelling in an old army Dakota air plane. When the plane had stopped for fuelling in Copenhagen, the head of the Froebel Training School in Denmark Jans Sigsgaard invited her to see a children's junk playground on a new housing estate in Emdrup Copenhagen. This Emdrupt playground had been in existence since 1943 when it was under Nazi Germany occupation. As Lady Allen wrote later:"In the moral confusion of German occupation the difference between sabotage and delinquency was not obvious, and many of the children had become unruly and antisocial. The Germans had no doubt encouraged this as a way of dealing with the apparent anti social problems they had with children.

Lady Allen later remarked,- "I was completely swept off my feet by my first visit to the Emdrupt playground. In a flash of understanding I realized that I was looking at something quite new and full of possibilities. There was a wealth of waste material on it, and no man-made fixtures. The children could dig, build houses, experiment with sand, water or fire and play games of adventure and make-believe." After her visit, on returning to London Lady Marjorie Allen remarked at the time "I knew in my first instance of seeing it that they had hit on something exceedingly extraordinary"."It is a rewarding experience for children to take and to overcome risks, to learn to use lethal tools with safety".

Later that year Marjorie published photos of the playground in Novembers Picture Post.

Picture Post special edition "Why Not Use Our Bombed Sites Like These".

The article showed photos of children playing in the rubble of the bombed sites and described the Emdrup Denmark junk playground. Following this Picture Post article there was a great deal of national interest in these new junk playgrounds. The result of which The "Under-Fourteens Council" through Lady Allen suggested the scheme for our big cities. Stating that, "Stepney and Shoreditch Councils have already reserved pieces of land for the scheme. Westminster has just bought two sites intending to use them as ordinary playgrounds. This seems to be a chance to try out the idea in another area where it is badly needed". *As a result a* variety of solutions were put forward and set up to take kids off the streets, which were seen as menacing, unsafe and breeding grounds for delinquency. Up till then the only planned and or designated play areas, had been the council controlled playing fields, recreation grounds, parks, hard tarmac and concrete surfaced swing parks. However the vast majority of children didn't even have access to many of these facilities, due in the main to increased traffic congested streets and busy roads which put limits on the child's journey. At that time (NPFA)The National Playing Fields Association had offices based at

Playfield House London were managed by a number of retired military officers and Drummond Abernethy. Drummond was someone Lady Allen had previously worked with and knew well. and had just returned to the UK having been teaching abroad and employed with the Rank organisation.

Lady Allen had read a letter in the London Times from A.S. Neil head of Summerhill free school fame, written from his home in Lyme Regis Dorset on the subject of juvenile delinquency. The letter read -"Granting that childhood is play hood, how do we adults generally react to this fact?.We ignore it. We forget all about it-because play for us is a waste of time. Hence we erect a large city school with many rooms and expensive apparatus for teaching, but more often than not, all we offer to the play instincts is a small concrete space. One could with some truth claim that the evils of civilisation are die to the fact that no child has even had enough play. Parents who have forgotten the yearnings of their childhood-forgotten how to play and how to fantasy-make poor parents. When a child has lost the ability to play he is psychically dead and a danger to any child who comes into contact with him". - A. S. Neil.

Lady Allen responded with another of her own 'letters to the Times.' stating that '- "Municipal playgrounds are often as bleak as barrack squares and just as boring. You are not allowed to build a fire, you would head straight for juvenile court if you started to dig up the expensive tarmac to make a cave, there are no bricks or planks to build a house, no workshops for carpentry, mechanical work, painting or modelling and of course, no trees to climb". *" That giving children opportunities to collectively play at cooking, building, and that clearly would work to eradicate those destructive energies that might lead some urban youth into delinquency".*

The King George Jubilee Trust report of 1952 'Citizens of Tomorrow' had stated that "children commit more offences on the streets than in any other place and everything possible should be done to provide alternative places, where children can play safely, freely and adventurously". "As a short term policy for meeting the needs of the present generation, it was worth considering whether, more of the bombed sites in the cities, could not be roughly fenced, lighted and provided with a lock up hut containing a variety of tools. So that children could have space and equipment to play games of their own invention". According to the (N.P.F.A) National Playing Fields Association pamphlet, junk playgrounds were "chiefly bombed sites where bricks, timber, and various materials have given the children a creative outlet for building walls and forts and generally exercising their imagination", and adventure playgrounds were "either a rough undulating site, probably an overgrown quarry, or a site that has not been cleared and levelled but which is left with its natural features- the children playing games over fallen tree trunks and up and down miniature hills and hollows". Natural adventure playgrounds either a rough undulating site, probably an overgrown quarry, or a site that had not been cleared and levelled, yet had natural features, the children playing games over fallen trees up and down miniature hills and hollows. The site's criteria requirement was of a playing area of one and a half to three acres with suitable play material for constructive play. Along with other (N.P.F.A.) National Playing Fields Association requirements of suitable, intelligent leadership and supervision, along with good separate toilets, drinking water, lock up hut for tools and undulating ground.

National Play Committee Formed

It was as result of the letters to the Times by A.S Neil and Lady Allen and the resulting national concerns that the very first committee of interested people from the world of child's play came together in February of 1953. Based at (N.P.F.A)National Playing Fields Associations offices in London's Playfield House. The group was spearheaded by the chairman of the newly formed Playground Committee of the (N.P.F.A)The National Playing Fields Associations Lieutenant-General Sir Fredrick Browning. Followed by Lord Luke. It consisted of four committee members of the Clydesdale Road Adventure Playground, Lady Allen of Hurtwood, Harold Marshall, Ruth Littlewood and Mary Nicholson:

Prior to this meeting the Mayor of the Royal Borough of Kensington had convened a public meeting in which approximately 200 people had attended. There were three speakers: Lady Allen of Hurtwood, Lord Luke of the (NPFA) National Playing Fields Association and Sir George Pepler, who was a town planner. At this meeting, the initial motion was approved to set up a national body to co-ordinate adventure playgrounds. Lord Luke offered the protective arm of the (NPFA) National Playing Fields Association for the new national organization.

Lady Allen at that time felt that the term junk playgrounds were worthy of a much better name to gain public approval. So prior to that first meeting at Playfield House, she had lunch with Sir George Peppler to discuss this matter in some depth and they came up with the name "adventure playgrounds". For the term "junk" was felt to be a drawback to gaining local authority funding and needed to be changed. The word "adventure" linked the playground concept with the ideals of the newly created Outward Bound Trust (founded in 1946), which provided young people with opportunities to undertake healthy outdoor activities and challenges thereby providing an important shift towards the importance of adult leadership. The term was seen as being more robust and according to Drummond Abernethy of the (N.P.F.A) National Playing Fields Association it was more readily acceptable to children. Marjorie wrote (N.P.F.A) The National Playing Fields Associations pamphlet Adventure playgrounds in 1953. So that by 1954, the (N.P.F.A) National Playing Fields Association had agreed and accepted that the term of "adventure playground" suggested by Lady Allen should be adopted.

During these first committee meetings at (N.P.F.A) National Playing Fields Associations Playfield House it became clear that while there was huge support for the scheme, most people did not fully understand the role of the play-leader. Lady Allen had strong mixed feelings about this lack of understanding, she knew that 'the right person was the key to success' and she wanted to see leaders properly paid. This was a problem because there was nothing to model this play leader role upon for it was a totally new position. Also there was at that time a general nucleus of feeling that although their hours were awkward- their supervisory responsibility duties were easy and many felt that the job therefore did not warrant a reasonable rate of pay. There were remarks at the meeting about people 'getting paid to just "playing with kids' which probably have started at about this time and often still continues so today. There are still some bodies where play workers are still paid an embarrassingly low wage and where their work is not valued These first play-leaders came forward in surprising numbers, yet were poorly paid. All these playgrounds were started by voluntary bodies with seventeen places opening. Just like the adventure playgrounds that they inspired the bomb sites had provided a wealth of junk materials and spaces for children's adventurous spirits. Children seemed to prefer the informality of dirt and scraps to formal jungle gyms. Eventually parents and park designers realized that these non-traditional materials inspired creative, thoughtful play. With the adults and children working together to construct the kinds of play spaces the children wanted. The playgrounds they built were not just play spaces; they were inspirations for numerous studies by child psychologists. Marjorie Allen -"it took many years to argue that an adventure play workers salary should be on a par with other social workers". She was concerned about qualifications and training. 'Good leaders with an instinct for following children's interests are born not made 'she says' 'but there are some skills that cannot be taught". " It is necessary that there should be a skilled leader who must be first and last a good democrat and not an autocrat. He must be an older companion in whom the children have confidence and whom they like. He must be an instructor, and an inspiration to those children who are timid and who are afraid to start on a project because they lack confidence. The leader must understand the different children and be able to ensure that the opportunities are fully used. He must have a wide experience of life and much practical knowledge. The leader must be willing to make each project a joint effort between the children and himself, where both have something to learn. The genius of the leader, of course, is to get all the children to work together by indirect suggestion. The children have to be secure in the knowledge that the place is their own, that the materials, tools and play equipment belong to them. The playground is a free community where the children play in small groups or join together for larger projects. The playground leader never organises groups or play. The leader has, of course, sometimes to help unravel difficulties, but the conflicts are in reality very few compared with those in other playgrounds". On the subject of a title for this person Lady Allen remarked "We cannot think of a good title for this individual: supervisor is wrong, connected in the children's minds with discipline; a play leader is trained for a different type of work, and for younger children, so we use the word 'leader' but it is not right. The role of the 'leader' is catalytic, and it is apparent from the various accounts of adventure playgrounds that too few adults have had to fulfil too many roles— from social worker to begging letter writer and woodwork instructor". An informal and changing group of people, both full-time and voluntary, and including friendly neighbours and older children is evidently the happiest combination.

As these first 17 experimental Adventure playgrounds were being established, there were attempts made by play leaders and others such as the (NPFA) National Playing Fields Association to clarify and define exactly what adventure playgrounds were. The N.P.F.A had sent a letter to all the local authorities concerned, pointing out that the playgrounds should offer 7 minimum requirements to operate. However, it was the definition from the Clydesdale adventure playground itself, which was readily accepted by the N.P.F.A as being the most appropriate. As a result the N.P.F.A offered a definition of adventure playgrounds through Mary Nicholson. These highlighted a distinction from what were referred to as 'creative, or junk playgrounds'. Mary was at that time Drummond Abernethy's personal secretary as well as being a close personal friend of Marjorie Allen.(N.P.F.A) National Playing Fields Association stated that the term adventure playground should describe a ground where tools and materials only are used, as distinguished from a ground provided with imaginative features, natural, which could have a distinctive title. Between 1948–1960 seventeen trial adventure playgrounds were established in the UK. Including those at Camberwell,

Clydesdale in Paddington, Ifield at Kennington, Lollard in Lambeth ,Shoreditch, St John's wood at Westminster, Shanty town in Notting Hill, others in the UK included Grimsby and Liverpool's Rathbone street. A (N.P.F.A) National Playing Fields Association Report into these 17 adventure playgrounds had stated that "leaders were often seen as eccentric supervisors, attempting to teach children destructiveness as a means of developing creativity in adolescence". Lady Allen-'It is evident that the help children get from the Play-leader is useful to them emotionally as well as practically, in a child's world a friendly adult who exerts a minimum of authority and is generous with his time and attention, maybe something of a rarity; and the children respond as if they have been waiting for just this sort of friendship". Lady Allen made the point that, although we use the word leader we want something different : "It must be a grown-up who exerts the minimum authority and is willing to act rather as an older friend and councillor than as a leader"." It is these children, particularly, who so deeply enjoy the companionship of an older person who is willing to be understanding and very generous of his time". "We cannot think of a good title for this individual: supervisor is wrong, connected in the children's minds with discipline; a play leader is trained for a different type of work, and for younger children, so we use the word 'leader' but it is not right".

Marjorie Allen with Lord Luke and Drummond Abernethy worked tirelessly to promote adventure playgrounds throughout those early years. The (NPFA) National Playing Fields Association started to offer capital grants and grants toward leaders' salaries for a two-year experimental period for each of two projects . On these early Adventure junk playgrounds the children used the materials already freely available such as bricks, timber, tin and iron. Materials which were there in abundance following the bombings of the former homes on these wasteland bombed sites. They used tools such as heavy hammers, pick axes, shovels, trowels, crowbars and wheelbarrows to carry them in or as carriers of bricks and earth. The children were always busily doing physical work building wooden and tin dens, brick walls and underground hideouts, though often these were crude and make do constructions. Lady Allen was not a great lover of local authority planners in those days as was seen when writing on adventure playgrounds-Lady Allen remarked, "They are decidedly messy occupations and they make the planners who are mostly tidied minded unhappy"."Nevertheless, they must never forget children enjoy being dirty and untidy, adults abhor it, we have to decide whether we are to make playgrounds for children, or playgrounds that please the planners". "The best the Borough Engineer can do is to level the ground, surface it with asphalt, and equip it with expensive mechanical swings and slides". " His paradise is a place of utter boredom for the children, and it is little wonder that they prefer the dumps of rough wood and piles of bricks and rubbish of the bombed sites, or the dangers and excitements of the traffic". "It is a rewarding experience for children to take and to overcome risks, to learn to use lethal tools with safety". *Writing on the differences of particular sites at that time Lady Allen commented- "Adventure playgrounds are significantly different from one another"."For they are influenced by the community, the nature of the site, the wishes of the children, the imaginations of the leader and the amount of money available".* She suggested that the adventure playground site should remain closed to its surroundings by a wall or fence, offering the fence as suitable because it provides children with privacy. Though many would say that it was to hide the un tidiness mess of the play dens and chaos from Adults prying eyes.

Marjorie Allen had been a major force in the development of adventure playgrounds and was helped by many others over the years, including Hon lady Anne Viney (Voluntary Secretary) and Marjorie Holmes (who took over the (LAPA) London Adventure Playground Association chair when Lady Allen had stood down in later years).

A glimpse into those times and the activities on some of these early experimental adventure playgrounds

London adventure playgrounds

Camberwell Adventure Playground

This was the very first officially recorded adventure playground in the U.K Save the Children Fund was the sponsor of the playground. Situated on the site of a bombed church which was known as Luke's or Rosemary adventure playground this ran from November 1947 with its official opening on 3rd June 1948. With support from the Under-14s Council and the Cambridge House Settlement, this playground ran till 1951 when the land was needed for redevelopment. A variety of waste material such as bricks, tires, rope, wood, sand and corrugated iron were left out for children to use to create dens, slides, climbing frames, furniture and anything that they could imagine.

The playgrounds chairman(Psychiatric Social Worker) George Burden stated in his playground report. "Finally, and most importantly, playgrounds such as ours set in a district which has suffered much during the war can lead a child away from the tolerance and approval of that destruction which is associated with the war. The child of nine or ten makes few moral judgments. He wants to do something and it is the doing which is absorbing, whether it is constructive or destructive, I believe he prefers to make and this is supported by our observations, but given nothing to make he will break. It lies in our power to assist him in choosing what is socially desirable and morally right. This playground is different because it's a place where the children have an infinite choice of opportunities. They can handle basic things — earth, water plants, timber — and work with real tools; and they have an adult friend, a person they trust and respect. Here every child can develop a healthy sense of self-esteem, because there is always something at which they can excel. The wide age range, from two years to twenty-three, is perhaps unique in any playground. There can be progressive development through rich play opportunities, to a growing sense of responsibility to the playground, to younger children and, finally, to others outside the play- ground. Their willingness to help others is the sign of real maturity which is the object of all who work with young people". -George Burden -Chair of Camberwell Adventure Playground (1948)

Clydesdale road adventure playground (Paddington)

Clydesdale road adventure playground opened on March 17,1952. It was created by Local neighbor Ruth Littlewood and Lady Allen. Ruth Littlewood had watched children playing on this bomb site next to her house and although it took a good deal of negotiation with landlords and hostile neighbours as well as fundraising it was eventually established. and was initially designed to cater for 5 – 10 year olds. However it soon became extremely popular with teenagers and very quickly there were a variety of activities available to accommodate all ages who wanted to play. The playground site was a ¼ acre with just a budget of £400 a year. The playground was officially opened, under the leadership of Peter Gutkind who had been recommended by Lady Allen. Peter with his fancy American style shirts soon gained an instant liking by the children with his energetic vision and enthusiasms. There *were* fights, particularly over the possession of tools, but real crises were rare. Indeed, it was often surprising to see how many activities were going on at close quarters, without serious friction, even when the playground was crowded to capacity. The youngest children might be riding a trolley down the slopes or digging in a somewhat aimless fashion with sticks or trowels; while the older boys were working at a pick-and-shovel excavation, the girls were playing some housekeeping game around the huts, and various mixed groups were making bonfires, or hammering boards or diligently helping the leader to construct a brick seat against the boundary wall. The Clydesdale playgrounds committee was joined by Lady Allen as its chair in 1953 and she stayed as its chair until 1963. She had convinced underwriters Lloyds to insure Clydesdale adventure playground as well as scrounging a Nissan hut for the playground. The insurance company was so impressed by the engrossed activity at the Cyldesdale Road playground, with its complete lack of hooliganism that it quoted lower rates than for an ordinary playground.

Ifield Adventure Playground - Kensington

The Ifield adventure playground which opened in 1953 was ran by local people with a grant of £3,970 from the local authority. Yet the playground was not recognized by the (N.P.F.A) National Playing Fields Association as being an adventure playground at that time in the true sense of the word; as it did not provide any of the facilities required for an adventure playgrounds social development. This was despite it being created whilst both the Rosemary adventure playground and the Clydesdale adventure playgrounds sites were still fully operational. It was seen basically as a bomb site where children played amongst the rubbish and this was obviously what they enjoyed. Here children swung on tires, climbed down ropes attached to ruined coal bunkers and walked around on the mud on stilts. The play leader was there to guide the activities, not to direct them. Children worked together to build a camp out of branches, boys lift large logs and girls passed branches up to the boys balanced on top of their construction. The adventure playground was closed in late December 1953 because it was regarded as being too rough.

In 1954 the existing conventional playground at Rathbone street in Liverpool was enlarged by an adventure playground and the employment of a full-time leader. However it wasn't until 1957 that Rathbone adventure playground officially opened. It was however soon branded the 'toughest' of all the English playgrounds. So many children crowded together on this adventure playground but statistically its slide appeared to be the highest risk. Whilst the permanent ironwork equipment generally produced more accidents than the junk and scrap materials in the Adventure Playground. The stories of gang-warfare abounded , sabotage, thieving scrap-metal merchants, hostility and indifference in the neighbourhood. Except for one street of immediate neighbours, senseless and wanton destruction was broadcast. There was poor planning and lack of solid financial support, in spite of mistakes made by its management and all its shortcomings. Many of which were said to be the result of hasty committee and the errors of its two play leaders . In spite of the roughness of the site, the endless brickbats, the noise, the dirt and the disorder, sufficient evidence has accrued to support the main thesis on which the playground was originally established. That given the tools, the materials, the adult interest, advice and support children will take part in constructional play, they do derive satisfaction from using hand and eye in making and building, fetching, carrying, painting and digging. From the start there was always fresh supplies of timber donated from local firms who called these deliveries Adventure play equipment. The Rathbone Street playground only seemed a failure from a distance and it soon led to further adventuring in Liverpool. Such as at Calderstone park adventure playground led by Gerry Kinsella and Jim Stanton who also provided opportunities for children with disabilities.

From the beginning of the adventure playgrounds in the UK, the relationship between the play worker and the child has been of great prominence. The earliest play workers, often volunteers, were responsible for play projects in the parks and were called

Park Wardens. The play workers' major roles were as enablers encouraging children to create things from waste materials. They were appointed as a means of providing some sort of constructive leadership to offset the children's gangs who were often involved in anti-social or juvenile delinquency. Childhood Gangs, seen as a major problem by the central government, had been prominent throughout and after the war years in each neighbourhood that was later involved in turning the rubble on the bombed wastelands into junk playgrounds.

The adventure playgrounds initially were run by voluntary groups of local parents and supervised by characters who had that special way with children. Notably, people such as Pat Turner, Harry Killick, Don Buck, Joe Benjamin and in later years Jack Lambert, Tony Chilton, Janet Dalglish and many others each had their own unique style of encouraging young people to create and work together as a community. These play leaders were providing an environment where children could do things which they were unable to do in any other setting. Here they could use tools to build their playhouses and structures from waste materials. They could light fires, cook, and use rope swings and aerial runways etc.

The idea was that the adult play worker and the children would work together, creating an environment the children really wanted. Lady Marjorie Allen, the major exponent of these playgrounds, remarked that children's love of freedom to take calculated risks is recognized and can be enjoyed under tolerant and sympathetic guidance. Children preferred these informal wastelands to any formally structured play provision. Often these places were seen as eyesores but within their environments, there was a discipline of their own making.

The play workers were often seen as Robin Hood figures directing the children away from anti-social street pursuits to more constructive and positive community outlets. Such people took the place of the street gang leaders mentality. Play workers were very poorly paid. They also had little in the way of resources. Depending on their own initiative, these first play workers, who were very resourceful and imaginative, were able to scrounge materials from companies, factories, building sites, or council housing demolition areas. Play workers had to be proficient at organizing play events, carnivals, trips out, and programmes as well as well as developing a good working relationship with the parents of the children and involve voluntary helpers from colleges and universities. With little financial help at first, the job was a challenge. However, these individuals attracted hordes of children to their sites which were often small strips of wasteland that had been the site of a bombed church or similar area.

In the mid-sixties, I had been appointed via Community service volunteers to run a new Easter playscheme at Redditch. Due to its success it was followed by my appointment by the council to operate a summer scheme. In later years I was appointed there as play coordinator for a 10 scheme programme, after training in Playfield House London Central, the new home of the National Playing Fields Association (N.P.F.A). N.P.F.A was at that time the main coordinating body promoting play provision in the UK and published handbooks such as Play Leadership and gave talks to local councils nationally to promote supervised play provision for all children. Whilst in London I was based at play worker Pat Smythes' Notting Hill adventure playground in Ladbrooke Grove in Kensington and Chelsea play association, home of the Notting Hill carnival and the steel band movement.

By the end of the 1960s, I was appointed by Balsall Heath Community Association to establish one of Birmingham's first adventure playgrounds in the heart of the city. I made contact with Gene Peck who had managed Birmingham's first adventure playground at Sparkbrook. This was to be, as the Bishop of Birmingham told me, my baptism by fire. Following those early days, I went on to establish numerous play projects throughout the UK, working alongside other play workers in Dulwich, Camden, Kensington, Deptford London, Stevenage, Skelmersdale, Bournemouth, Redditch, and Rogerstone/ Gwent.

The special relationship between play workers and children is paramount for the success of any play project. Some people have a particular flair for working with kids: a natural ability which cannot be learned through any training programme. Many play workers had this special gift. The social administrator of Balsall heath once remarked: "The streets can be empty, not a child in sight, but then Ray Wills comes along and suddenly hordes of kids appear out of the alleyways and houses as if by magic from nowhere." Specific examples of the play worker child relationships include the ability to relate to very small preschool children as well as the teenagers. A special ability to relate well to these groups is essential. We worked with the kids on the streets in a detached role initially prior to working the sites. This way we established a good working personal relationship with the kids in the area then we could encourage them via trust and empathy to work with us as a team on the playground. The leader must know when to help a child and when it was best to withdraw so the child was able to work out the problem alone and thus learn self-confidence through unaided personal achievement.

As Jack Lambert Welwyn garden city play worker remarked,"It comes down to this, I am not a leader but a servant to the children."

CHAPTER THREE

FREEDOM TO PLAY

Children playing on a typical adventure playground - The Venchie

When a child has lost the ability to play, he is psychically dead and a danger to any child who comes into contact with him. — A. S. Neill,

"Play is a very personal experience. For some it is dolls and fights, for others it is climbing and skipping. It is what children do when adults are not there or what the children do when the adults that are there are perceived as honorary children." Bob Hughes

"The child without the playground is father to the man without a job."-Joseph Lee.

In ten years of experiment there was not one serious accident on any adventure playground whereas by contrast during the same period the architect designed play area in Camden claimed weekly accounts of broken bones, fractures cuts and bruises". It was said at the time that "The cost of one adventure playground leader's salary who supervised up to 100 children at a time is less than the cost of one child in Borstal". Lady Allen was able to declare that "After more than 20 years, ' no parent has ever made a claim against an Adventure Playground". It was always with leadership, for without supervision and the enabler of the play leader, it was no longer play leadership. The relationship with the kids was always the essential criteria and the most vital factor. It was during this period that the play leader employed to supervise the playground was established as a key figure and took over the responsibilities formerly covered by local volunteers. During these years a variety of adventure playgrounds operated and were established in cities throughout the breadth of the UK. These are some of them and their success stories.

Lollard Adventure Playground Lambeth London

Harry Killick the Lollard adventure playgrounds first leader

Lollard opened as a playground in April 1955 and ongoing works started to construct play equipment and build huts for classroom and winter activities. Formerly the site was a bombed out school and it had also previously been used as an unofficial dumping ground for refuse of all kinds and consequently was known as "The Dump" or "The Ruins". Marjorie Allen had wanted the site to be used as an adventure playground for obvious reasons. "Lollard was well placed to be used as a demonstration project since it is within walking distance across the river from the house of commons".-Lady Marjorie Allen. "Visits from MPs would be easy to manage and the place would be a constant reminder to Government of the need for children's rights to be paramount". The (LCC) London County Council agreed to a peppercorn rent and to fence the area. Although the local residents had been calling for the site to be used as a playground, only two of them would volunteer their time to serve on a committee. The rest would readily complain whenever anything went wrong. Parents and neighbours struggled with the untidy aspect of the playground: rubble, a mountain of clay, and unsafe tunnels belonging to the old school. Many would have preferred to see a formal and green playground there instead. Lady Allen says that she felt that they 'did not make clear enough before the site was created, exactly what an Adventure Playground was'. Lady Allen and some other volunteers were eventually gathered together to establish The Lollard Street Adventure Playground Association and put together a constitution. The Lambeth Council, the National Playing Fields Association and the Greater London Playing Fields Association all contributed to the project. The playground management team was joined by Drummond Abernethy of the (NPFA) National Playing Fields Association. Some neighbours complained about the untidy, smoky and noisy site (the nuisance caused by the children waiting for the playground to open), others approved it. With so much time and energy invested in its publicity campaign and to spread the message about the benefits of Adventure Playgrounds, the playground site now found itself inundated with journalists and TV crews. The children enjoyed this for a while but eventually it interrupted their work/play activities.' 'Lady Allen found the press coverage that Lollard received, mixed in content and quality. Her main messages were still simple. " A massive supply of materials and a resourceful and sympathetic leader". During that time Lady Allen had an old caravan situated on the site.

It consisted of an adventure play area, hard surface area for ball games, and an area for moving equipment and a toddlers play area with an assistant. They managed to get hold of an old Nissan hut at the playground which proved expensive to reconstruct at a cost of over£1000. However it provided access to lavatories, electricity and indoor play space, a tools store, carpenters bench and books for the children. A rarity in times of austerity with rationing still in place. Even for most children to have access to books was a rarity. The children painted the hut and the signage and took great pride in it. The girls cleaned and swept the building, because they chose to, and outside all the kids began digging and building and demolishing and cooking on fires it looked a mess. Lollard Street adventure Playground kept the interest of older children and young people up to the age of twenty thus enlarging the scope of possible projects. The older boys built and equipped a workshop and eagerly sought to serve the community in which they lived, doing repairs and redecorations for old people in the district, paying for the materials from a fund of their own. These were the same young people who are such a "problem" to their elders.

The Chairman of Lollard summed up lollard street adventure playground-"This playground is different because it's a place where the children have an infinite choice of opportunities. They can handle basic things — earth, water plants, timber — and work with real tools; and they have an adult friend, a person they trust and respect. Here every child can develop a healthy sense of self-esteem, because there is always something at which they can excel. The wide age range, from two years to twenty-three, is perhaps unique in any playground. There can be progressive development through rich play opportunities, to a growing sense of responsibility to the playground, to younger children and, finally, to others outside the play- ground. Their willingness to help others is the sign of real maturity which is the object of all who work with young people".

Gradually over time the playground's became accepted by the community. Harry Killick its leader was a local dad who was said to be quite a character both in personality and dress. A vivid description of him was published in an article in the weekly magazine, 'Illustrated" of 26th November 1955. The article stated that "he was a man with no pretensions- just a knack of handling children from the smallest Lambeth child upwards everyone calls him 'arry. He is a bulky, happy man with a turned up nose, spectacles like Billy Bunters, a rumpled shirt, a tear in his trousers and army boots laced with string'. Nothing annoys Harry. Nothing hurries him. He is diffident with prim little girls, as large men always are he is on terms of understand and level friendship with the tough little boys and the faintly hostile older ones. He laughs all over his broad face if you suggest he 'understands' the children. 'Nobody understands anybody else' he says' I think I just sympathies with them".

Each day Harry rode to work at the playground at Lollard Street on the most fashionable form of transport of that period which was of course a motor bike. He was often to be seen talking with the children of the neighbourhood, being a brilliant story teller of adventure stories of pirates and highwaymen. These stories were in vogue during that time in the popular Children's books and comics. Harry had to work with a difficult neighbourhood and attended regular committee meeting. Which consisted of locals, signatories, service men and council officials. Harry took a great deal of criticism from the locals and was often inundated with good ideas from these over helpful committee members. The playground not only attracted school aged children but also wee tiny totters as well as older kids already in employment. On one occasion these youths said they wanted to build a sandpit for the little ones, they worked hard to construct it and then spent a couple of weeks playing in it themselves. Lady Allen remarked at the time that she was ' glad that these tough young men were catching p on a pleasure that they had missed. An adventure playground is about the only place where that can be done.'

There was never enough building materials at the playground and it gladly accepted all kinds of free donations. The children tried to build a play mountain when loads of top soil were dumped onto the site, however this consisted of London clay though for a time they enjoyed the pottery and making mud slides, but many of their clothes were ruined and the clay just had to be removed. An old life boat arrived and soon was well used along with an old van which was dragged about the playground for sometime before it broke. Despite all the complaints that the Adventure Playground was dangerous, Captain Bratt of the (NPFA) National Playing Fields Association and the treasurer of Lollard, managed to get Lloyds of London to insure the site for claims up to £50,000 for £5 per year. Lloyds were 'impressed by the fact that a responsible adult was with the children and by the argument that children deeply engrossed in play were in fact less likely to have accidents. Than children who are driven to boredom on fixed conventional playground equipment in ways for which it was never intended.

In 1956 Lollard published a pamphlet which addressed the issue of the aesthetic appeal of the playground in this way: "Can the playground be made to look attractive? It depends on who is looking at it"."People who would like it to be always tidy and always the same will be disappointed. Too much is going on", "the main attraction will be the sight of children enjoying themselves." Sheila Beskine a teacher from the local secondary modem school, was one of the voluntary helpers at the playground at that time and edited Play leader the newsletter of the National Association of Recreation Leaders. Harry eventually left the adventure playground, no doubt suffering from burn out after working long hours in a stressful job for very low wages and trying to bring up a family at the same time. He was replaced as the adventure playground leader by Joe Benjamin, who despite his obvious ways with kids and his radical thinking only stayed at the playground for a short time before moving on in 1957 to run a new playground in Grimsby. He felt that Lollard adventure playground was run with too much outside interference and there was not enough involvement from local people. This criticism was held to be true by Lady Allen.

Following Joe Benjamin departure from the playground it was taken over by the legendary play worker Herbert S Turner or as he was best known Pat Turner a former schoolmaster soon made his mark. When Pat took over he had been told, "Unless you can do anything with it, the place is doomed." Pat soon was to encourage all manner of community involvement, Pat later wrote a book based on his experience at Lollard called 'Something Extraordinary". "The intensity of these little ones is a joy to watch, their affections like their movements are direct and spontaneous". "A hand slips into mine and slips out again, some purpose has been served, some other purpose now demands attention".

Pat set no rules, but clear standards for the playground. The children listened to classical music maybe for the first time whilst he played the violin as he wondered around the site. He encouraged the kids to be involved in the wider community, thus breaking down many of the barriers between the adventure playground and the locals. One of the many activities he encouraged was the national popularity for camping in tents and cooking meals over open fires. This was important in a neighbourhood where many parents were working and the kids came to the playground at lunchtime and cooked their own meals. The children went on to produce a newspaper and an operetta! The under fives had a supervised playgroup session funded by The Save The Children Fund. When Donne Buck was appointed as assistant play leader in 1958, he developed a garden growing flowers and vegetables all year round. The playgrounds activities included cooking around open fires, camping, gardening, sketching, jiving along with poetry, firewood services for the elderly and furniture repair services.

The only disadvantage at Lollard was the youths reliance upon Pat. His relationships with them were profound for many of them looked up to him as some kind of father figure, friend and confidant. When Pat left his successor was expected to carry on a spirit which had died, and she was not to blame that she could not control the acts of vandalism. She could only have achieved it by employing new helpers and gaining many new children. But the popularity of Pat along with the loyalty of the youths, plus the fact that she was a woman, made it nigh impossible to achieve. Visitors came to the playground frequently during this time and spent hours before leaving keen to start up new playgrounds. Then one night the hut was burnt down. Its lease ran out in 1960 and it was closed and another school was built on the original site. Some time before 1977 it moved from its original site, now occupied by the Lillian Baylis School, to a site on the main road that was used by Ethelred Youth Club. In 1985 the playground moved again and today it has an extensive system of raised walkways, odd free-standing stage-like structures and a bouncy bridge made from sheets of rubber.

At Shoreditch in London in 1956 Donne Buck started up an adventure playground. Situated on a site which had previously been in use some years earlier, but had been left abandoned with just a few tools in a garden shed. Donne remarked - "Nevertheless the children came in droves and had a great time playing with broken bricks and demolition timber, digging underground dens and lighting fires, making gardens, finding "monsters" etc – good basic stuff." Meanwhile in St. John's Wood Westminster London another adventure playground was about to be established which opened In 1957. Its lease being signed by Lady Allen of Hurtwood as one of the initial signatories and it was built on the site of former terraced houses that were knocked down to make the existing housing estate. It was intended to be a nursery but became an adventure playground instead and local Children were involved in its initial design and planning. In the same year The Triangle Play Association established the Triangle adventure playground at kennington London. So named due to the triangular shape of the site. Founded in 1957 by the late Marjorie Porter and it remains the oldest adventure playground in London and one of the oldest in the UK. Marjorie was awarded an MBE for her work with Lambeth's children and was still attending the playground's management meetings at the age of 96. She died aged 101 in January 2009.

The Notting Hill Adventure Playground Association founded Shanty Town adventure playground at Telford road Notting Hill London in 1958 to deal with the problem of the unequal distribution of parks in the Kensington area. Lady Allen of Hurtwood opened the site specifically as a way to encourage and facilitate children of different races and communities to play together. The area had had a variety of social problems and issues throughout the 1950s as a result of sub standard housing "Rachmanism", racial unrest, poverty and lack of space. The development of play provision was also seen as a way to deal with these anti social problems, social unrest, racial tensions and overcrowding of the area. By uniting the community in a common purpose through adventure playgrounds run by local people. Summer projects had instigated by Rhaune Laslett a community worker who was born in the East End to a Native American mother and Russian father. She involved local people bringing together up to 200 people at a time to work as volunteers on play schemes, free schools and adventure playgrounds. It was soon to develop into one of the largest community projects in the UK. The adventure playground was managed by an executive committee of a voluntary association which included representatives from the London Playing Field Association and the (LCC) London County Council. The LCC had approved grants of £!,700 via their education committee to cover staffing and running costs. Rhaune Laslett at one time joined forces with the steel band leader Selwyn Baptiste to teach children to play the steel pans at the adventure playground. The adventure playgrounds first leader Pat Smythe, was a former paratrooper he was assisted by Francis McLennan. (In later years Francis led Angel Town adventure playground).Within a decade the adventure playground had gained a national reputation as a fine example of a good playground, staffed by competent and professional play leaders. The adventure playground, was visited by Muhammad Ali at the time of his return fight with Henry Cooper and the 1968 Notting Hill Fair/Carnival concluded at the adventure playground with an 'open air dance and benefit gigs for the Neighbourhood Service at the Roundhouse which included acts such as the Small Faces, Sly and the Family Stone, and David Bowie.

At Grimsby its adventure Playground located in Armstrong Street in the West Marsh neighbourhood was run by Joe Benjamin. It had originally opened in 1955 and was surrounded by a high-wire mesh fence, close to Bennett's large timber drying shed and the paper mills wood pulp storage sidings. It was known locally as 'Shanty Town' due to its huge assortment of dens and houses created by children out of waste materials on an extremely very muddy site. Joe Benjamin remarked. "There was a large wooden creosoted hut at the far end of the site where tools, screws, nails, etc, were kept and handed out by the site supervisor" and sometimes jumble sales were held . Shanty Town was popular with the pupils of the nearby Armstrong Street School and a large slide was made by them in one corner, using corrugated iron sheeting, railway sleepers and lengths of timber. Timber, screws, nails etc were donated by Bennett's' timber merchants, who had their sawmill next door. Children, after climbing a ladder to a height of about 12ft, would sit inside a large galvanized metal bathtub and then slide quickly and noisily down the makeshift slide, flying off the end and coming to rest on the soft ground. Although most dens were built above ground, some were dug underground to represent a submarine, with a pile of old lorry tires on top to replicate the conning tower, with a ladder sometimes reaching 6ft below ground level. "Scrap cars and lorries were left on the site for children to play on and provided hours of play for would-be racing drivers." However, Shanty Town was not to everyone's liking as in 1956, people living nearby branded it 'a scandal and a disgrace'. With 56 of them signing a petition for 'the abatement of this nuisance'. However, at the same time, another petition signed by 252 people in support of the playground was handed in at the town hall and the council decided not to take any action.

The children created a variety of elaborate huts over time these were named by the children and included the "White Hotel, "Estate Agent", "The Cop Shop" and "The Fire Station" complete with home-made ladders. There was also "Shanty Town Hospital", manned by a staff of three Red Cross lads, a girl of thirteen and two very junior orderlies aged eight and nine years. Joe remarked "The medical staff built a waiting room onto the hospital and have produced their own blanket and armchair. They are also making a stretcher. The hospital staff took over first aid, the fire department patrolled the various bonfires. At the 'Cop Shop' police arrested wrongdoers and tried them in open court". In all these cases, the initiative had come from the children themselves. Joe Benjamin- "At the end of each summer the children saw up their shacks and shanties into firewood which they deliver in fantastic quantities to old age pensioners. When they begin building in the spring, "it's just a hole in the ground— and they crawl into it". "Gradually the holes give way to two-storey huts. But they never pick up where they left off at the end of the previous summer. It's the same with fires". "They begin by lighting them just for fun. Then they cook potatoes and by the end of the summer they're cooking eggs, bacon and beans. Similarly with the notices above their dens. It begins with nailing up 'Keep Out' signs . After this come more personal names like 'Bug hole Cave' and 'Dead Man's Cave'. There is an ever-changing range of activities "due entirely to the imagination and enterprise of the children themselves . At no time are they expected to continue an activity which no longer holds an interest for them. Care of tools is the responsibility of the children. At the end of 1958 they were still using the same tools purchased originally in 1955. Not one hammer or spade has been lost, and all repairs have been paid for out of the Nail Fund." Joe Benjamin left in 1959 shortly before the adventure playground was closed in 1960.

At a large meeting of play professionals in 1955 adventure playgrounds were defined as being, children, a site and a play leader. With the play leader making all the difference for he is the humanizing element, the person who brings the whole thing to life.

The majority 8 of the 10 experimental adventure playgrounds in London were closed in 1960 and the properties were redeveloped. Whilst four were open part-time, five were operating full-time (three financed and administered by local authority parks departments, two financed by local education authority and administered by independent committees). Some other playgrounds opened in temporary sites as short-term experiments. Some places were damaged because of inadequate fencing and then closed or transformed into other types of play grounds. In 1956, Drummond Abernethy was appointed to the (NPFA) The National Playing Fields Association with a brief to promote play leadership and adventure playgrounds nationally. On each of these adventure playgrounds over time children gradually developed skills in using tools, hammers, saws, along with basic engineering and structural skills and imaginative creativity.

Another UK City, Bristol had established a variety of adventure playgrounds throughout the city in the 1950s and 60s. One of these based at Lockleaze had evolved from waste ground at the end of Romney Avenue in the late 1960s when a local couple helped children build dens and swings. Its first two play leaders were Stephen Trevor Smith and Richard Evans. In 1972 two teachers and pupils from the local Lockleaze Senior School took a petition to the town hall to obtain council support and it received gained grant aid from Bristol city council that year. Shortly after Film and TV star John Cleese officially opened the playground and it was given the nickname "The Vench". It is now an open access playground and offers a wide range of activities like ramps, football, swings, and retains activities such as digging, or building dens.

Adventure playgrounds were also established in Scotland during the early 1960s, including within the cities of Edingbourh and Glasgow.

At Craigmillan in Edinburgh the Venchie adventure playground was established in 1961,situated between the Wee Free Church and the University Settlement building at around 63 Niddrie Mains Terrace. It was originally established by the work of Jim Brunton. After he toured Seden and Denmark where adventure playgrounds had been in operation for almost 24 years. It was originally known as Niddrie and created by Edingburgh University Settlement, making it possibly the first adventure playground in Scotland. It was part-funded by the local residents group and the University Settlement where many of the early volunteers came from. The local parents ran Beetle Drives and a 'numbers racket' using the Sunday Post football scores. Play activities on the site included den building as well as being rolled down the small hills in wooden barrels and playing in old cars. Before play structures of railway sleepers and telegraph poles were introduced and used by the children. Another popular activity was webbing. There were army surplus webbing belts, liberally adorned with metal studs and chains which they used for fighting. Seeing how fast they could whip the belt off and hit the wooden poles (stand-ins for other gang members). The first play Workers were Ozzy and Jaffa Popperoffski a married Israeli couple. In later years through the 1970s it was very successful when led by popular play workers Ron Aitken and Ron Crosbie. Save the Children Fund had managed and funded the scheme (with some grant aid from the local authority) from 1967 until 1998. In preparation for the handover a steering group was formed of local people, representatives from community based organizations, businesses, and local parents . From the initial steering group the Venchie Management Association was created to take over the project from Save the Children and to run it as a successful community facility. For 40 years, the 'Venchie' (as it is known locally) has been widely used by generations of local young people.

Whilst at Easter House in Glasgow the Venny adventure playground- based in the notorious Gorbals was opened in 1964. After the young folk singer and local man Matt McGuinn persuaded the council to set aside a former council rubbish dump for the site. With a grant of £1000 a year to employ Matt and 2 assistants. An old Nissan hut was set aside on the site for indoor activities along with rope swings and ladders, car tires etc. Providing a haven for hundreds of kids though it soon had gained a bad reputation for bullying. In 1966 Following a visit by councillors its grant was taken away. This however caused a public outcry from local parents and a march to town centre was organized in which over 500 children took part. As a result the site was saved and the yearly grant was increased. Other adventure playgrounds were developed in Glasgow throughout the 1960s and 70s. These operated through Glasgow Play Association. The play workers 2 young Americans who became very popular amongst the children. Frankie Vaughn the singer entertainer had visited Easter House community around that time 1968 to quell the fear of juvenile gangs and to encourage youth facilities. By 1977 the Strathclyde District Council had decided that it could no longer support the adventure playgrounds in the city. This meant that the two adventure playgrounds no longer received grant support and had to close.

In St Pancras -London the council opened the Parkhill Adventure Playground in the 1960s to serve the many young families moving into the area. Mike Buckley was one of the very first adventure playground leaders in Camden and was responsible for setting up the adventure playground. After moving from Birmingham to Gospel Oak to work for Camden Council's social services. *Pathé* newsreel entitled 'Adventure Playground' filmed the playgrounds. "this new form of childhood play area would bring a sense of adventure amongst the "high flats" of the city". "The idea is to encourage children to be constructive, so that city life means more than bustle and dangerous games in the street." It is a "toy-town-world with a purpose": to "learn to enjoy themselves, and to enjoy learning." The activities available to the children, who pay 'thruppence' for upkeep, include the hiring of bikes; peddle cars and the use of an adventure playground. Whilst the boys build large structures with planks of wood, and park their peddle cars at the 'petrol station' for some light mechanical maintenance, the girls in the adventure playground are isolated to a wooden shop, selling paintings to each other. The playground later had high rope walks and perilous structures. In 1971 a group of young artists had created a one-off six week "holiday camp" on the bomb site at Talacre for children's use in the summer holidays. Care of Ed Burmans Inter Action Trust. Here Adults made barbecues and built play areas among the rubble and debris. The community loved it and it was repeated in 1972 when a group of unemployed actors created e a people's pageant. Talking with local people, they found a strong desire amongst them to keep the open space. The council planned to demolish the slum houses in the area and rebuild on the site. When locals began to ask why they couldn't keep the space open after the demolition the actors created the pageant as a campaign. The council officers, however refused to listen as they wanted to built housing right across the site, leaving no green space at all. A film director heard about their campaign and made a film, which was called "The Amazing Story of Talacre" which was covered by the media. The actors and the people marched to Camden Town Hall to demand the space be kept from development. Camden council agreed that the people of Kentish Town could have their open space. As a result an adventure playground was built there in 1974 and planning permission was granted to use the site as an open space in 1975. Mike Buckley was promoted to head of Camden Council play services. The adventure playground closed for a number of years then re-opened in 1986 and today is run by Camden Council as a play centre with term-time after-school clubs and holiday play schemes.

At Wandsworth in 1967 it was recognized that there was a desperate need for an adventure playground and this was planned with the support of Social workers, (IVS) International Voluntary Services and Wandsworth Community Venture. As a result The

Wandsworth Adventure playground had had its official opening in July of 68 with the celebrity Jeff Astley present. Their first leader Diane Newton had been appointed then and she quickly made her mark. Setting up clubs for all age groups along with an Under 5 play group.

BIRMINGHAM

Between 1948 and 1953 several pilot projects were established in Birmingham. The City Council developed Adventure Playgrounds with staff assisting children to use waste wood and other industrial by products to construct their own play equipment. Then in 1954 Birmingham Parks Committee Education Department operated a successful adventure playground scheme between June and October with a voluntary group of teachers supervising the playground then later appointing a male play leader. However it was not until the 1960s that full time adventure playgrounds were first operational in the city at Sparkbrook, Handsworth, Balsall Heath, Hockley Port h along with a variety of play centres at Mount Street Recreation Ground, Nechells and Sparkbrook. In the following fifteen years, a further ten sites were opened though some of these were temporary 'Summer holiday sites. All of these operated on an open access basis, and were free of charge.

Gene Pecks Sparkbrook adventure playground

Play tower at Sparkbrook adventure playground pics courtesy of Geoff Galforth.

The initial proposal for a an adventure playground at Sparkbrooke was presented to the council by the Sparkbrook Community Organiser. With both the site and funding provided by Birmingham council (via the city parks fund). The playground was officially opened in 1965 in Sampson road and its very first play leader was Gene Peck. Gene was a young man who it was said of at the time had considerable ability and was soon to make his mark. Showing that running an adventure playground was more than just keeping kids busy and off the streets. Street youth gangs instead of becoming a menace were soon to discover a new role of importance as members of the adventure playgrounds community. In his first playground report in 1962 Gene stated that there would be up to ninety to a hundred children at a time using the playground daily. Geoff Galforth assisted Gene for these years often on a voluntary basis.In the early days all the activities were on site ubtil a play hut was established there for table tennis and other indoor activities. Social activities included wood sawing for the childrens homes a bonfire in November and numerous parties and fund raising activities. Although initially den building was encouraged especially during the busy summer holidays. Initially there were flimsy where gangs of teenagers met. A nursery group was established for the small children run by locals Mrs Osbourne and Miss Kent.

1965 was the year of the first Sparkbrook Carnival, forerunner to the Balsall Heath Carnival, and also largely a product of Gene Pack's idea and energies. The playgrounds contribution was a galleon created by the children and aptly named 'The Adventure,' which won first prize in the float competition for Sparkbrook community association..

The playground was also recognized at the time as playing an important role in "countering racial discrimination by giving children of all ethnic backgrounds the opportunity to play together". The adventure playground at Sparkbrook became an important part of the lives of many of its children particularly those of the Irish community. The adventure playground closed in later years.

Due to a need for more space what was called an adventure playground reopened on Farm Road on 31st May 1968 and local children were given an hour off school to test the soundness of the equipment before the Whitsun school holiday commenced. Hundreds of children took part in the shooting down slides, scaling climbing frames and swarming over the play dome. Though this was a purpose built area and with no loose parts or adventurous activities. It was no way an adenture playground in the true sense of the world. Its first leaer was Brian Popplethwaite. As I relate in my next chapter of this book in 1970 I took some my playground kids from Balsall Heaths Malvern street to visit. They were not impressed with the ironmongery and no dens etc.

Playing on a den at Sparkbrook aventure playground

Fairstead estate adventure playground 1970

CHAPTER FOUR

MY EARLY DAYS IN PLAY

Art Picture courtesy of Dawn Jeanette Grant Harrison
What an extraordinary adventure

*We built those big adventure playgrounds in those pioneering
days
we used the best of timber constructed great walkways
the kids came from the neighbourhood from two to twenty one
they swung upon those Tarzan swings oh boy did they have fun*

*The streets were full of laughter in those bye gone days
when the kids did all gather there to while their days away
there were tiny tots and punks with bikes skin heads and greasers
too
little kids in fancy dress and kids with just one shoe*

They built their wooden dens there and painted them real cool
there were tall beams with commando nets
with ramps and slides a few

The games they played were roustabout run out and give chase
there was laughter on the playgrounds then with smiles upon
each face
we used big tools and hammers with saws to cut and prime

There were hordes of children playing there all having a special
time
the leaders all wore long hair and the kids were satisfied
no health and safety limits then just common sense and rhymes.

Ray Wills

I entered play work through Community Service Volunteers in 1966 which had its offices in Toynbee Hall London and I worked on a variety of placements in the UK. As male nurse with Barnard's at Earlies children's hospital, Housemaster at Witness manor boys school in Kent, Play leader at Rumford and London central Y.M.C. Venture Weeks, Assistant at Loaning head boys home in Cumbria and then as holiday play scheme leader at Redditch. At Cumbria I was taught to canoe and to swim by Olympian champion Lindsey Williams son of Revd. Williams who ran the Cigarillo home for delinquent boys from Newcastle. (Based loosely on the ideas of A.S Neil).

Rumford YMCA Venture weeks were the idea of Ray Oxen bridge its leader at Rumford Y.M.C.A in Essex. Here we operated a variety of play activities at the centre for children, including the usual table tennis, badminton, dressing up and team games and numerous trips out throughout the school holidays. During these weeks we escorted large parties of children to London Zoo where the kids were allowed to hose down the elephants and watch the chimpanzees tea party. On a visit to the Queens Household cavalry in the children were allowed to give sugar lumps to the

Queens drum horse Anselm. They were able to handle the guards equipment in their barrack stores and to watch the horses being trained there. The scheme culminating in a summer camp joined by London central YMCA held at Battle in Hastings/During the end of camp sports day Here I won the leaders mile race and was carried around by the children who called me Hippy due to my long hair floral shirt n beads.

It was later whilst with C.S.V that I was placed at Redditch and I had my very first experience of operating a new holiday play scheme. Working for Redditch District Council, under the guidance of Bill Pilcher the park superintendent. Here I was responsible for their first Easter holiday scheme in the Beoley Road neighborhood, with its old terraced red brick council houses. This scheme was operated from the local recreation grounds with use of its own football pavilion. It provided me with an excellent opportunity to involve local people in the events and play activities, in organizing day trips out to the seaside resorts of Rhyl, Barry Island and Blackpool. Children's parties were held at Redditch towns Kingfisher hall community centre. I visited the home of and invited the local Roman Catholic clergyman, in his long black smock to referee our play scheme football matches, whilst my assistant play leaders, organized recreational activities involving a large number of local children. The very young children who came to the scheme took part in the toddler's fancy dress show and preschool activities. The older children organized a firewood delivery service for local senior citizens, with council support. With it being such good weather and a hot holiday period the scheme proved to be well attended and was therefore very successful. On completion of the scheme, Bill Pilcher the Redditch councils parks Superintendent, called me into his office and asked me if I would like to return again in the summer, as an employee of the council. He informed me that the council had offered to pay for my attendance at a play leadership course run by the (N.P.F.A) National Playing Fields Association at their headquarters at Play Field House in London. I was overjoyed to be offered this opportunity and soon made the necessary plans for the trip to London. I was to attend the training course in London under the guidance of Drummond Abernethy at Playfield House. I had previously read the books on play written by Lady Allen and Drummond Abernethy and produced by the (N.P.F.A) National Playing Fields Association.

The adventure playground at Ladbrooke Grove in Notting Hill was to be the highlight of my first time in the city of London. Here I worked under the guidance of the Senior Play leader Pat Smythe and here I was to learn at first-hand about the benefits to children from their involvement in adventure play. At that time it was an amazing experience working on a playground where leaders and children were busy sawing and hammering, constructing neat play houses. Whilst others swung from ropes or tires and straddled rope netting on high wooden towers. There seemed to be something happening here all the time with a child's allotment area and a pets area. A small bonfire supervised by children with regular visitors from film companies. Including the cast of the west end show Oliver and the local police providing car rides for the kids in their panda cars. Donne Buck had also spent time here previously following his Adventure playground successes at Shoreditch and Lollard Street Adventure playgrounds.

Notting Hill adventure playground

At the Notting Hill adventure playground there were large tall wooden telegraph pole towers straddled with ropes, commando nets, and rubber car tires. Here both black and white bare footed children were everywhere, children of all ages all mixing freely, playing happily together, all their run and chase games across the tops of towers. Whilst others were involved in a variety of delicate balancing acts in between the tall wooden telegraph poles. Throughout the site there were a large variety of (well-constructed) wooden, miniature playhouses, along with numerous forts and camps. All created, or else being built by staff such as Francis McLennon and the children. All of these were in various stages of construction. There was the constant noise of children's raised voices of laughter and chattering, along with their hammering and sawing. Plus an occasional swear word, when a child missed a nail, or hit a finger(his own or another child's)with a hammer. I noticed that more elaborate miniature wooden houses were neatly constructed by the children, with the guidance of the play workers on the site. Teaching the children practical skills in carpentry with the correct use of saws, hammers and nails. In the far corner of the site there was a pet's area with a nanny goat, along with the rabbit's hutches with bunnies all tenderly cared for in their solid built homes. Nearby there was a well-tendered small garden area, containing pretty flowers and a variety of salads and vegetables neatly lined out. Later in the evenings we were treated to the unmistakable musical sounds coming from out of the long galvanized tin shed, situated in the far corner of the site of the local Caribbean group. At that time it had its own Caribbean steel band, with the Caribbean sounds of the steel drum pans echoing across the neighbourhood, which rehearsed in the tin shed in the rear corner of the site. No doubt influenced and guided by steel band leader Selwyn Baptiste. Playing distinctive sounds from their hammered out, crude man made steel drums, no doubt busy practising for the forthcoming Notting Hill Carnival. The site itself was brim full of events and activities daily. In the brick play hut the small children were involved in painting sessions and numerous active indoor games, along with action rhymes, and outside group games such as pond and bank. Here toddlers to youths congregated freely, whilst a large blackboard outside the office displayed in hand written chalk by Pat Smythe its leader, displaying the days main programmes of activities. The play staff and volunteers were often crammed into the small office within the play building for meetings, discussing local issues and ordering play materials by phone. The local police arrived in their panda cards and took the kids who had queued up for hours, for free rides around the neighbourhood on a regular.

Within a decade Pat Smythes Notting Hill adventure playground and Francis Mc Lennon's Angel Town adventure playground had both acquired national reputations. As superb examples of working adventure playgrounds. Pat Smythe leader of the Ladbrooke Grove adventure playground was a local man and former paratrooper. Pat remarked(1968) after having been on the Notting Hill adventure playground site for nine full years as leader-"The atmosphere is homely to the boy, returning from a spell in Borstal, to the old age pensioners coming to their own club". "To the unmarried mum bringing up her baby, to the nursery groups that she herself attended not so long ago and homely to the West Indian youth fresh off the boat"."Homely to the thousands of children who had come in off the streets". On a visit to the Notting Hill playground by Arvid Bengtsson with members of the (N.P.F.A.) National Playing Fields Association that same year. Arvid when commenting in later years on this visit remarked, "I do not think that I have met anything since my first visit to Emdrup in 1946 that has made me so thrilled"."It has just the spirit and atmosphere I have always been looking for in my playgrounds, but I did not find out how it was achieved". Many more Adventure Playgrounds were founded at this time, but Notting Hill is the longest established Adventure Playground in the borough of Kensington. (Pat Smythe was in later years to be very active in the area as a local Labour party councillor). Here at the Notting Hill adventure playground I was aware that there was so much going on, on the site and off the site and its influences were profound, vibrant and exciting. It was amazing to me that so much was happening there, within such a small confined playground site. Here older children were busy looking after little ones, maybe a young brother or sister, others playing energetic ball games, building dens, or playing chase. Older gangs of youths boys and of girls, just looking on, chatting or involved in building relationships with their peers, creating their

64

imaginative dens, or involved in some other robust activities. Always questioning the decisions of others, challenging, energetic, physical and most of all very involved and absorbed in some activity.

At the time I also was instructed to visit and assisted at other play projects including the brilliant Battersea adventure playground at Wandsworth. with its busy aerial runways and slides built into play mounds. (There is still footage somewhere online of me with my long hair and flared jeans assisting the kids there).Also at Holland Park adventure Play Park and One O'clock club.

Holland Park adventure play park

Drummond thought that it was vital for me to see this scheme for as he said he wanted me to see what Pat Turner one of the original adventure playground leaders had achieved with the establishment of these One O Clock clubs. I recall attending a small Child's birthday party in the play hut at Holland Park Play Park One o clock club and singing happy birthday to a little boy,

65

accompanied by the playgroup leaders piano playing. Here I was taught finger play rhymes after being introduced to the kids and staff by the play group leader as being one of Mr Abernethy's lads.

The influence of Drummond Abernethy

At this time at Playfield House I was to gain friendship with W D (DRUMMOND) ABERNETHY (1913–1988). Former teacher, who had previously worked for the Educational division of the Rank organisation and was Secretary to the International Playground Association (1963–1972). He worked for (NPFA) The National Playing Fields Association from 1956–1977 where he was head of the Children's Play Department. He was also a member of numerous national and governmental youth organisations. At (NPFA) National Playing Fields Associations Play Field House and throughout the next thirty years he was to be instrumental in my understanding and grasp of the important values and philosophy of Child's play work, the discipline and the profession. Drummond came from a background in teaching. His contribution to Child's play was profound in every respect; he was unique and highly respected throughout the world of play. Drummond was a distinguished gentleman, silver haired and always immaculately dressed, as well as being a superb orator and spokesman for the play profession. Drummond gave regular talks to local authorities community groups and others in his role of Director of N.P.F.A both within the UK and also on the continent. These were always high in substance as well as content, very informative and exactly executed. Drummond was always available and supportive and was always keen to talk with me on all aspects of play issues. His view of adventure playgrounds was that they were the "hub of the community". By this he meant that the playground "must be part of the whole community and be involved in every aspect of the life of the people making the community". "It is not a separate entity, nor is it in competition with the Youth Service; rather the play leader is cooperating with all leaders, teachers and parents and is a friend and helper of all children, teenagers and tiny tots". *I was told by Drummond in the late 1960s that many of the forerunners of these Children's national charities such as the Pre School Play Association, Under 14 Council and The Central Council for Physical Recreation were initially established at Playfield House.* In 1965 Drummond wrote in Town and Country Planning, that "Children and teenagers are not delinquent, but the products of what we have done to them when they were small. Moreover, this is a period when the sanctions have been thrown overboard and when teenagers are strong and virile group with little to do with their ample leisure. Recreation must fulfil their needs, if action is not taken not only will a child's development suffer, but also they will in all likelihood turn to anti social activities". Drummond, had advocated the provision of specific space for child's play within each community, close by and within their own neighbourhood. "Somewhere to run, shout, climb and a puddle to splash in, a place to dig and most important of all a place where a play game could be shared with another child. Play spaces in which children could share their wonderful games and their flights of imagination, for these are their birthrights. If children are denied such places, for trial and error, they become withdrawn, or timid and set back in their own development and never regain lost ground".

Drummond was to influence many within the field of play throughout these decades. His contribution to Childs play was profound in every respect; he was unique and highly respected. He was a distinguished gentleman, silver haired and always immaculately dressed, as well as being a superb orator and spokesman for the play profession. Drummond often told his many audiences at his ever popular speeches on Adventure Playgrounds, that despite their appearance looking like chaotic undisciplined environments. That within these spaces there was actually a discipline which was a self imposed discipline within the children which was not imposed from outside. It was this which was lasting with many effects on their life with immense benefits. A discipline that evolved out of their play which was more real than any imposed from outside. As Drummond was always saying "Children want and need to play, they cannot help it, and it is in their very nature and necessary for their full mental physical and spiritual development". "They should always be

67

encouraged to play, for not only does it keep them happy, but also they learn so much through their play experiences". "Children have always played from time immemorial. " Drummond read out 2 statements about problems with youth and then said that there were not modern concerns but these two statements were from Greek and biblical times.

He once remarked to me at one of our regular chats "The adventure play leader is to be seen like the captain of a ship". " He must be in charge of the playground and not be subservient to his management committee". "For his adventure playground to be successful, he should know through his contact with the kids how best the playground should operate and then advise his management committee accordingly". During these times and for many years after I attended the numerous play leaders meetings held at Playfield House mixing with all the play workers and pioneers of the play movement. Throughout the years Drummond and I continued to communicate by phone, letters, often meeting up at play conferences and his occasional visits to the Adventure playgrounds I was responsible for. We would often exchange ideas and information on all aspects of Child's play. For at that time we were both keen to see the establishment of an Institute of Play Leadership encompassing both the playground workers and the play leadership staff. As well as to see more integration of the disabled children on adventure playgrounds. Drummond Abernethy had been secretary of the National Playing Fields Association Playground Committee since 1953 until his retirement in 1978.Then he acted in an advisory role. Drummond's energy and vision at that time led to the establishment of numerous play projects nationally and throughout Europe. Initially he had played a significant role in refining Sorenson's ideas into adventure play, speaking to local authorities, play bodies and community organizations. Thus over the years he had become a known as an astute accomplished and formidable spokesman and orator on the subject of play leadership in general. As Drummond Abernethy was so fond of saying regarding children and their play "they have always done so from time immemorial." (N.P.F.A)The National Playing Fields Associations Playfield House was at that time in the mid to late sixties still staffed by retired officers of the armed services. Many of whom I had got to know personally in the years ahead and throughout my play career. These included Lieutenant-General Sir Fredrick Browning ,Lord Luke, Captain Wicksteed, LT Col Bob Sautherwaite, *Captain Tony Way, Major Tatham and Captain Forbes.* I had earlier been employed in previous years as an officers batman at Bovington Army camp working at the Bovington RAC Officers Mess. So in many ways working in a military style establishment was not new to me. During my weeks on the training course at Playfield House I was placed on a variety of numerous play projects to gain experience and in insight to the play leadership philosophy in practice. My main base was at the Notting Hill Adventure Playground. It was there that I worked under the direction and supervision of Pat Smythe and alongside Francis McLennan for a few weeks in the hot summer school holidays. After my time with (NPFA) National Playing Fields Association at Playfield House was over I returned to Redditch. Where I was now employed by Redditch District council to run what was to be a successful summer holiday play scheme on the Batchley estate.

Then following my time in Redditch, I was for a while assisting the Warden Rob White at Carey school camp in Wareham, Dorset. A camp established by Dorset Education department. Catering for 120 school children per fortnight. As well as scout guide and youth work clubs. Here I was responsible for guiding the children in outdoor pursuits, overnight camping expeditions, orienteering and recreational pursuits as well as campfire sessions. It was whilst I was there that I received a phone call from Drummond Abernethy of the (N.P.F.A) National Playing Fields Association informing me that Elizabeth Dickinson Wellington councils play organizer was keen to employ me there to manage at one of their play centre's at Donnington. Drummond told me that he thought that I could do a good job there. At Donnington Salop under the guidance of the play organiser of Wellingtom District Council Elizabeth Dickenson. I was responsible for a busy 11 âcre recreation area which contained a thriving play centre as well as numerous playing fields. This project was so very busy, situated as it was close to a very large housing estate. I ran a wide range of sport and leisure activities and programmes. I was also responsible for a thriving busy youth club as well as a club for small children from the centre. One of the youths who assisted me there was taken on in later years under my recommendation to run the scheme and others in the town. It was following my success at Wellington Salop that I applied for the post of adventure playground leader for Balsall heath in Birmingham (for adventure playgrounds were my thing and where I really wanted to work).

CHAPTER FIVE

THE VENTURE

Art picture courtesy of Dawn Jeanette Grant Harrison

"It is a source of experience which the child can tap freely and at will, without compulsion, restriction or commitment, the child learns to live, work and play free, friendly and in a self disciplined way"- Tony Chilton, Leader of Blacon / Chester Adventure Playground;

City Backstreets.
I remember the city backstreets
the alleys where the kids did play
the rows of terraced houses
the street light across the way

I remember the cobbled streets
the little alleyways
the girls with curly hair
the cold and bitter winter days

I remember the tat man
the coal man who would call
the streets were full of laughter
the bouncing bats and balls

I remember the city bullring
the mount pleasant hill we walked
the weekend ride to Malvern hills
the brummies and their talk

I remember the Ladypool road market
the Indian bazaars
I loved the Cannon hill park
the tulip festival and boats
the zoo and BBC pebble mill theatre
in my head I took these notes

I remember the skinheads
the lads who loved to play
the adventure playground was full then
in the summer holidays.

Ray Wills

I had applied for the post of play leader for Balsall Heath
Community Association in 1969. Following my interview at the
local Clifton road primary school in the autumn of 1969 I was
appointed shortly thereafter. The Balsall Heath Association
offices were situated in the Mount Pleasant Community Centre
adjacent to the U.Ks first comprehensive school. Where Gwen

Blandford of the Balsall Heath Association worked as school counsellor. Balsall Heath was a socially deprived inner city area, multi racial, with red bricked terraced corporation housing. Contrary to the accepted story I was in fact the first leader and I established the adventure playground at Malvern street. Until my appointment the adventure playground did not exist. The chosen site for the playground was an abandoned piece of wasteland in Malvern street. Overlooked the rear premises of a nail factory, backing onto a public house, a row of council house backyards and a railway bank siding. The Balsall Heath experience for me was to become my training ground for what was to follow in my career in play-work. Here I was to work closely with alongside community workers employed by voluntary bodies, church groups, local council etc. From organizations such as The Cadbury Trust, Shelter, Council Of Churches and the Church of England Society. Many of the streets of Balsall Heath were narrow, some still of cobbled stoned (old Balsall Heath) alleyways. There were many wastelands in between the terraced houses, mainly as a consequence of the councils continuing demolition of the many slums in the city. Many families were hoping to be re-housed in the Chelmsley Woods area at sometime in the future, though for many this was still just a dream. The area had its own Muslim mosque at mount pleasant road and a popular market stalls parade in Ladypool road. The ladypool road market was a beautiful setting for such mixed cultures, here one could buy anything from Indian sari cloth materials to a wide range of Caribbean fruit and vegetables. Here there was also a shady side with child prostitution and roads such as Woodstock road which was a red light district for prostitution. Crime was also prevalent though most of it petty, though there were car theft and house burglaries along with common assaults usually upon the Asian community. Petty crime amongst the young was seen as a cultural problem. (just like the country child scrumping apples) Whereas here the kids tatted from empty houses, which was stealing copper and lead wire etc. Then selling these items off at the local (tat) or scrap yards or they stole items from the market stalls in ladypool road. Many of these were involved in illegal merchandise, collecting copper tanks, stripping wiring, boilers or car batteries. These were then taken to the local scrap yard merchant, known locally as the tat man, for pocket monies. There were stories in the press of babies eaten by rats, or left abandoned in phone booths by young mums. Along with stories of kids on the run from the authorities. Nearby the Moseley area was well known for its drug culture and student population. Here in the inner city area there was an abundance of very large families Irish families, along with much social neglect and deprivation.

On the first day on the job and I was to my initial contact with the street kids of the community on a damp winter cold evening. I stood where the street lamps shone outside the site. A small group of teenage lads were idly playing a game of dare, each trying to edge on the others to smash the street lights with nearby handy pebbled stones. Whilst they ran in and out of the wasteland, as they did so, playing a sort of adhoc game of chase. I stood in the shadows watching them for a while and then when they became aware of my presence I strolled over and introduced myself. I recall telling them of my appointment and of my desire with their assistance to build an adventure playground on this wasteland. I told them that I hoped it would be a place where they could meet regularly, build camps, dens and hideouts. To build play structures of timber for climbing and swinging from. A place to light supervised campfires and cook. But most important this would be their place. The lads sported shaven heads as was the fashion (skinheads) they told me their names .I noticed that they constantly spat as they talked, perhaps an indication of their street credibility in this area of the city where kids had to live up to their reputation. In sharp contrast to them I was just a few years their senior and a country lad with long shoulder length hair. During my initial period at Ballsal Heath I tended to work on the streets in a detached role, getting to know the local kids, community leaders and building up contacts with the kids as well as the community leaders.

Whilst I was at Balsall Heath I was to hear of a variety of other adventure playgrounds across the UK. Adventure playgrounds which had either been established or were just in the process of establishment across the UK. Including that of Mint Street

Adventure playground in Southwark London. Mint street Park was once occupied by the original Evelina Children's Hospital and in 1970 local resident Moira Scully began a campaign to get the redundant tram tracks behind the former hospital lifted and an adventure playground or as she put it a "rough and tumble" playground built on the site. She was ably supported by Ellis Blackmore the local curate from St George the Martyr church and other local parents. Including Ted Bowman, who was part of the campaign to get a dedicated place for young people. Together they set up the current adventure playground with its building and staff base. Story has it that the actual site was at one time a workhouse of which the author Charles Dickens based his workhouse in Oliver Twist. Another new adventure playground Hornimans site had also just sprung up in London operated by local volunteers, on the site of an old coal merchants. This site was to have a variety of kids-designed structures together with customised fixed play equipment, with many buildings, a central street with camps for girls and boys on either side and a unique earth pizza-oven made by the children. The playground was to keep goats, rabbits, guinea pigs, cats and ducks and developed an environmental pond and garden. Another new Adventure Play centre Plumstead at Greenwich London SE10 was in operation built on a former quarry and dump site. The design of the playground was also conceived in consultation with children within a continuous raised circuit, enabling the children to remain off the ground until they leave. The circuit included small beginners swings at the start, progressing to a challenging Round the World at the end.

At Birmingham I lodged for a while in a co operative house in Handsworth shared alongside Margaret Parker the Balsall Heath Associations social administrator and her friends. I would also visit the offices of Mount Pleasant community Centre where the Balsall Heath Associations own office was situated. There I would meet up with youths I had got to know at the nearby Mount Pleasant Comprehensive playground nearby. On one occasion breaking up a fight, between youths on the hard tarmac playground as I knew all the kids involved by then and already had a relationship with most and was accepted as" he's ok". Often in the evenings I would walk the dimly lit streets of old Balsall heath with Margaret Selby the Council of Churches community worker, on her regular visits to meet up with local families. Here the kids of all ages would play skip and ball games on the cobbled stoned streets and alleys in the light of the old street lamps, between the rows of terraced corporation houses. Here there was always lots of noise of kids voices, parents arguing and dogs barking till late at night. The terraced houses were all of close proximity to one another and people tended to know all their neighbours private business. Despite this it was very neighbourly with large families of children and folks supporting one another with babysitting or loan of tea etc. Often there would be sounds of broken glass from a window smashed by a child's ball, followed by a chase by an irate neighbour. Child prostitution was also apparent in the area alongside the poverty. Other lads would play ad hoc games of football on any free piece of land or street corner there were very many of these where kids played. In the winter they would be involved in yearly Guy Fawkes tradition, seeking donations on every street corner, or gathering outside newsagent shops with shouts of "penny for the guy, mister" conker games were also very popular then. During these cold winter months kids would make go cart from discarded prams and sheets of tin sledges used for sliding down the severe steep mount pleasant hill to the mosque below, which was the first in the UK . Snow ball fights and sledging were also popular then at Edward road outside the police station in old Balsall Heath and down the very steep Mount Pleasant hill. Many kids then would often take part in more adventurous and somewhat dangerous pursuits such as exploring the many abandoned empty houses where electrical wiring and glass was in abundance . The dangers to children were a concern with the risks of falls, accidents, or the health risks of infections like impetigo, which was caused by the intense demolition dust of the area. One morning I was laying in after a long night with the youths and visiting families when I received an unusual visitor. Revd Loundes brought a visitor to see the Venture all the way from new York in the USA where they were at that time looking into developing an adventure playground there and the guy wanted to talk with me and to see the Balsall Heath playground in action.

The Malvern street adventure playground was to become a place where kids could let off steam and release their energies constructively, an escape from poor housing, poverty and social neglect. The playground soon became the place to build camps and dens, somewhere where the older kids at one time built tall wooden forts containing a brick chimney fireplace. Here they cooked meals of spuds on the open fires and entertained friends. Wooden ramps were created, zigzagging across the site, for games of chase across constructed earthen play mounds. Scattered around the site, hordes of local children created small wooden dens, both below and above ground. Many of these were ingeniously constructed and contained hidden trap doors and underground tunnels in abundance between all the dens. Many of these were built on warm summer days or evenings and often treasured in the cold winter months that followed. Such a place was the Malvern adventure playground which consequently took the name" The Venture", so christened by its users and became a local kids meeting place. Here children of all ages, colour and creed, gathered together with me around communal bonfires during cold winter months, burning potatoes and roasting their fingers. It was here they would chat whilst watching snowflakes fall often into the dark evenings. This was a place where they congregated to hear local gossip, banter and make new friends. Many chatted freely about thing that were bothering them at home and at school. I now lived nearby in Clifton road lodging with the Warren family, Alan and Margaret with their boys, Mark, Anthony, Trevor and Michael. Their house back yard overlooked the playground and it was here where I stored the playgrounds many tools, hammers, saws, wheelbarrow and play equipment. Such essentials which were used for playground construction of forts, dens and play structures. The nails for the playground were kindly donated from the local nail factory in Hereford road, which backed onto the playground itself. Many students from Birmingham colleges and universities along with reps from numerous student organizations visited Balsall Heath regularly often as part of their training and worked for voluntary bodies and volunteer organisations. The adventure playgrounds had many visitors included the Bishop of Birmingham, who christened the playgrounds leaning tower, this was made from wooden duck board palettes, the Bishop called it "The tower of Babel". The Bishop turned down my invitation for him to attempt to climb it though. He jokingly told me that my appointment as leader of the playground in Balsall Heath was no doubt a baptism of fire. As play workers on our adventure playgrounds we were often seen as robin hood figures, particularly so in the socially deprived areas of the cities often taking the place of gang leaders. I have worked closely with leaders at adventure playgrounds who had little or nothing in the way of resources, or finance and very little management support. But who attracted hordes of young people and developed superb adventure playgrounds from just a small strip of land despite the obvious financial or limited resources available. They were however very resourceful and imaginative, such qualities which children took onboard. Adventure playgrounds and play projects need to have dedicated and imaginative individuals who can bring fresh ideas, challenges and opportunities to local communities through the Child's adventure play movement.

The local clergyman the Revd Bill Loundes from his church St Barnabus at Ladypool road was now a regular visitor at the site. To so many of the kids he was a sort of uncle figure, greatly respected and admired .This was especially so by the skinhead youths, due to his appearance with his wearing of bovver boots, and his craggy looks, grey beard and long black cloak. Bill Loundes would often be seen walking the streets of the community, visiting families, often late at night and often out in all weathers. In the snowy winter months he could be seen reading his large bible, sat on the bench in the grounds of Moseley local park and oblivious to the severe weather conditions and snow blizzards. Margaret Selby the community worker was very active in the area and in later years was to become Dame Margaret Selby and Dean of Aston University. Both Margaret and Bill were great encourager's to me and supported me during this time and we become very good friends. At the playground I was involved with the children in their building of dens, towers along with organizing games or just chatting and there were many play projects organized including trips out and visits to their family homes. Often these visits were in the evenings, where I was always made most welcome by the children's parents, many of whom were to became close friends. I particularly recall families such as those of Margaret, Sharon and Mandy Carey's household, these were Irish protestant origin. These were very pretty little girls who always shadowed me everywhere, even to the Birmingham town centre Y.M.C.A hostel at canal street, where they often stayed for tea or had a cooked breakfast in the canteen. The Donnelly family were also of Irish descent, catholic, with roots in southern Ireland and I would often be invited to their home in Clifton road for supper. This was particularly refreshing after a long day at the playground and at one of the many youth clubs I led. This was also the case with many other Balsall Heath families. Numerous social workers came to visit the adventure playground during those times, including those who were on placement from colleges. One social worker lost his car keys and wallet at one time but these mysteriously reappeared following my chat to kids from old Balsall Heath. A that time Professor Dick Atkinson worked in the area Dick had a major influence on its future housing development though not directly involved with the adventure playground. Strange characters would turn up unexpectedly on the adventure playground like the maladjusted young man who was seen as a kind of village idiot at first mocked by the kids and yet was quickly accepted. Many student volunteers assisted me in numerous play projects in Balsall Heath throughout the year. It was always my dream to set up a new adventure playground. For me it was a challenge to work on an empty waste land with just a very few resources, with no assistants, little monies available and in a socially deprived community. Like all the early adventure playground leaders at that time I worked alone and had to depend on my own resourcefulness and I had to become adept at managing and involving people from the local community. To become clever at persuading companies building sites agents, factories and stores to give freely in the way of timber, materials and donations of food etc. The communities in which we worked had endured bombings of the war years, rationing and the slum clearance measures which in fact destroyed much of community life and neighbourliness, which was unique. For many of us who took on these challenges were untrained, but we had an inbuilt desire to work with and within the communities we happened to be placed with. We lived there locally in these neighbourhoods and so became excepted by the locals and particularly by the kids. We knew that we had to built up a close affinity with the kids before actually working on the site. Many of us chose to work in a detached role a few months or so prior to commencing work on the actual site. Visiting local clubs, schools and on the street corners where the kids congregated. So we were able to get to know many local kids well and involve them on the adventure playgrounds establishment from the very start so it was theirs. A regular visitor and volunteer at the playground was Mike Halward from the Birmingham branch of (IVS) International Voluntary Services. Mike spent many months assisting me on the playground and in the wider community and became a close friend. Another close friend and play worker who assisted me on a regular basis at Balsall Heath was Brian Shaw.

My idea for the Malvern Street playgrounds very first community bonfire and fireworks event was well received by the kids and local parents, youths and children were all involved. I scrounged food and presents for the Guy Fawkes competition from local shops and monies for fireworks was donated by parents and local traders. On the day of the event in excess of 200 people were in attendance and many parents took on the responsibility for refreshments and the supervision. All of the (B.H.A) Balsall Heath Association committee were in attendance that night along with many local community leaders and it was quite an exciting evening. The area of Balsall Heath included neighbourhoods stretching from Moseley village including Sparkbrook. It consisted of old Balsall Heath with its old slum areas of red bricked housing bordered by mount pleasant with its new community centre, mosque and comprehensive school. Moseley road had its old municipal public baths, the churches of St Paul's, Church of Christ, St Barnabus church and the Indian picture house. During my first winter at Balsall Heath Des Wilson from the Shelter organisation was introduced to me by Margaret Selby. I took him around the many houses meeting up with and introducing him to families whilst he shot pictures of their housing conditions for his forthcoming Shelter Report.

The Seeney family lived in old Balsall Heath neighbourhood and following the tragic death of their mother with a brain tumour the local social services department stepped in and had plans to separate the children and put them all into separate care homes. However the kids thought otherwise and didn't want to be separated. For quite a while they were on the run from the authorities, hiding out with help from their friends and neighbours. Unbeknown to me at the time they spent many evenings hiding out on the adventure playground in Malvern Street being fed and cared for by one of our playground regular Michael Warren. Eventually there was a public outcry and a led by the national press The Daily Express culminating in a Cornish family taking them all in on their farm with an newspaper headline article entitled "Kids in Clover". Their story was later made into a film "The Fourteen" or" The Wild Bunch" starring Jack Wild as Reg Seeney and June Brown who was in later years to play Dot Cotton in the famous popular TV series Eastenders. It was filmed in London at the Notting Hill adventure playground at Ladbrooke Grove in Kensington.

During one hot summers day I arranged an outing for all the kids to the Birmingham Tulip Festival at Cannon Hill Park in Sparkbrook. After a great deal of heated phone discussions with the local (N.P.F.A) National Playing Fields Association office and the support of N.P.F.A s Drummond Abernethy in London I was given free admittance to take a large party of 200 children to the event courtesy of Birmingham Corporation. I was privileged to escort the group through the street of Balsall Heath and then downhill to the park. It was a bright hot sunny day and one I will cherish, when children from the poorer areas of the city were able to enjoy the occasion of the city festival. Despite the large numbers of children we had few problems, many parents came as supervisors. At the festival the children were thrilled by the motorbike riders who rode through flaming hoops and to see all the tulips on display. We did lose one small boy but he was safely found in the lost children's booth and quickly rejoined us. During my time at Birmingham I also attended numerous Play meetings at the Handsworth Adventure Playground which had opened a year earlier and which at that time was going through many difficulties with vandalism in the summer and winter of 1969. Its present leader John Huff spent many hours at my home in Clifton road and on the Balsall Heath Adventure playground. One Sunday I was invited to bring the playground kids to a special televised service of the BBC 1 TV programme Songs of Praise shot at St Paul's church Balsall Heath. In the morning of that day I collected them from their homes, around 80 in all and escorted them to the church in Moseley road. The new modern vicar welcomed us and we were led to the front of the church and the children sat on the floor in front of the aisle, much to the embarrassment of many parishioners as many of the kids were poorly dressed and looked a motley crew. They joined in the pop style modern Christian hymn singing and were actively involved in the service by the vicar. The construction of the play structures on the adventure playground could involve work parties from local colleges or universities and students from voluntary bodies, such as 'The United Nations Association' or 'International Voluntary Services.' The adventure playground had now become a vibrant and exciting community of children of all ages and abilities.

In the autumn a small young local boy Billy Jevons went missing and there was a wide search with TV and media coverage. The search led by my next door neighbour Mrs Pat Henry one of the playgrounds mums. Eventually Billy was found by a local Indian lad, who had gone searching riding the area on his push bike. He found Billy sleeping beneath a tree in the park at Moseley and Billy's family were greatly relieved. The lad on the bike was interviewed on national TV, he said that I should have been interviewed and not him. I visited Bills home shortly after Billy was returned home and his parents became close friends. One particular Christmas time, when I was staying at the Birmingham Y.M.C.A hostel at Snow Hill and a member of their social committee I planned a party for 200 kids at the Y.M.C.A hall, these children were from the poorer parts of the city. I brought along some 80 children from the adventure playground and I compeered the event. Another community project I established was to make use of a deserted former dentist's surgery, as a meeting place for local youths which was a detached house on Ladypool road. What to do about the problem of skinhead gangs had become a major concern and big issue by the local press courtesy of Birmingham Mail. With a high profile on the problems of these detached youths who did not join the traditional youth clubs in the city. There was a regular section in the local paper The Birmingham Mail at the time on "The Detached". With the support of the Revd Alan Wright the playground chairman I met up with many of these youths and persuaded them to assist me on this new project. The empty house in Ladypool road held lots of possibilities and was soon to become a major success. Initially we visited the neighbours close by the house and told them what we were doing, before digging up and tidying the back garden of the property. The youths cleared the rubbish from the building, all the water, gas and electricity services were put back on, floorboards repaired and a coal fire was lit and floors carpeted. The local police were welcomed to visit and given mugs of tea, along with other visitors including local members of the clergy and community leaders. A local tramp was made welcome by the youths and would often sleep overnight. The local skin head youths played darts, cards and chatted here for many hours throughout the long winter. During this cold severe winter when the snow and ice was deep and whilst assisting as a receptionist at the Lane Neighbourhood Centre with Margaret Selby. I was asked by Margaret to help deliver Xmas parcels to local residents. This was part of a national appeal by the national newspaper The Daily Express I was assisted by the youths of the area in this project and we were soon delivering parcels to needy families.

Children growing up in such communities had to contend with many illegal attractions and temptations and so often the lifestyles in such communities encouraged petty crime as an acceptable way of life and so often these areas were a breeding grounds for delinquency. Once the child has a police record or were on probation they are prone to get caught up in the wider world of crime. Thus often the young offender meets up with others and criminals who are more heavily involved. If the young offender is not deterred and his circle of criminal friends is not broken away from he will most probably drift into an unhealthier lifestyle. Leading eventually to stronger sentences. Therefore the need for more positive healthy pursuits from an early age is paramount ways needed to be found and avenues to direct them to more constructive and positive pursuits to enhance their childhood years. The adventure playground concept was in my view one of the best means of achieving this by encouraging young people to seek constructive outlets for their vibrant energies and throughout their leisure periods.

Early each Thursday morning, I would call at the home of the Revd. Bill Loudness at St Barnabus rectory in Woodstock road. Invited to attend, special large cooked breakfasts with percolated coffee in the company of a variety of community leaders. These breakfast events would often last for hours on end. Here many local and national issues were discussed, these were often heated debates. Here I sat alongside other community leaders such as Canon Schiff, Margaret Selby, Revd Trevor Rowe, Revd Alan Wright, Revd Bill Loundes, Gwen Blandford and Mrs Loundes. Later I was involved in a "March of Faith" parade from Balsall Heath to the Birmingham city centre. Here we would attend a special open air service where all faiths and religious denominations joined together in prayer. Each Christmas Balsall heath held its own carol service parade around the streets of the neighbourhood. Stopping outside the public houses and specific dwellings to sing carols. This was an evening event involving all the various churches with the church leaders carrying tall lanterns and all the kids of the area would join the parade to St Paul's church and other churches locally.

CHAPTER SIX

BALSALL HEATH ADVENTURES

Malvern street adventure playground

Old Balsall heath

On the cobbled streets of old balsall heath
where the children skipped with dancing feet
where the lamplight shone o'er darkened skies
where the lonesome strangers passed on by

on the streets and shadowed alleyways
where the dogs did bark and children played
where the dust was thick and illness spread
where six children laid n shared one bed

where the Senney mum died of a brain tumour
where her children ran hide from the law
just fourteen kids all on the run
from foster homes and carefree mums

they hid within the playground dens
where the play some poet laid his pen
where barefoot urchins ran the streets
amongst the demolitions of dark damp streets

the children nicked their breakfast rare
amongst the multiracial Fayre
where Pakistani and Caribbean crew
shared their life amongst the brew

the law gave chase and papers spoke
where wise men read of kids elope
where public cry was heard so plain
across the streets of Birmingham

eventually the law awoke and let those kids to Cornwall slopes
where farm was rich in love and flowers

here the children shared a life 'neath boughs
no more to run the streets so bare
loved by the farmer's wife and cared.

Ray Wills

We now had a permanent play building on the adventure playground with its costs donated by the playgrounds patron Paul Cadbury of the Cadbury Trust. The adventure playground was now well established with a strong membership of regulars and an active parents group along with strong links in the community and a wealth of resources. The local community became aware that something very special was happening here. Social workers, church leaders and visitors came from as far afield as the United States to visit the adventure playground. Many visiting Birmingham were told "you must see whets happening at the adventure playground at Balsall Heath". During the days on the site we held regular camp building contests with prizes for best built dens particularly during the summer months and the adventure playground resounded with the sounds of children hammering and sawing right into the evenings, creating a vast number of dens and small wooden boxed miniature houses. The Matthews brothers Sam and Robert were always regular attendees from the start. A group of children from the playground went with me to Wales at the log cabin Rowntree Trust centre and others went on a trip camping with me in the grounds a house in the lake district courtesy of Birmingham Social Services. Occasionally I took children on days out to visit the Notting Hill adventure playground in London. It was at one of these (APWA) Adventure Playground Workers Association meetings. That following a long discussion the members voted on changing the name of our title or role on adventure playgrounds from play leader to that of play worker. As in many ways the job on the adventure playground was so vastly different from the play schemes or play centre's leaders role which was more about recreational games and sporting activities were as play workers on adventure playgrounds were more of a community workers role.

The Balsall Heath adventure playground was fortunate at that time to receive a gift of a large tall towering Dalek, (popular in the BBC TV series of Dr Who). This was donated by the Birmingham students carnival committee and was operated and lit up by a large car battery inside and this soon became very popular amongst the playground users. Obtaining regular supplies of building materials for the playgrounds den building and play structures was a constant need at that time. We were dependent on the good will of the Birmingham's city corporations demolition gangs who delivered wooden beams and floorboards prior to their dismantling of the slums. Parental support for the playground and its activities was strong considering all of their housing difficulties. During my time at Balsall Heath I had been fortunate in developing a reputation of somehow attracting hordes of kids. People like the B.H.A Social Administrator Dick Empson had said that if I was on the streets hordes of kids would suddenly arrive as if from nowhere, as if by magic and I was seen as a kind of pied piper. This was not magic however, but years of effort in meeting kids on the streets, building relationships and trust, in their family homes, schools and on the play projects.

A strong parents support group was formed which met in the Edward road police station in the old part of Balsall Heath with support from the police community Relations officer. This trust and support of the local parents was instrumental in the playgrounds success, as was the help of volunteers and local traders. At that time I was also active in old Balsall heath assisting with the formation of one of the country's first Free schools and a holiday play scheme which was run by (IVS) International Voluntary Associations student groups. Students had been regular visitors to the area over a number of years. Some of them providing temporary holiday play activities, adventure playgrounds and wild west shows throughout summer school holidays. Games of cowboys and Indians were extremely popular and many small campfires were created throughout the school holiday on the playgrounds and also on the other wastelands in old Balsall Heath.

Cobbled Streets

We danced and played the cobbled streets
hard brick and stone beneath our feet
our homes were terraced all in line
red bricks back yard and washing line

Our lights were gaslight our rhymes were free
we played games in our street so merrily
we spun those tops and ropes of string
we hopped and skipped around the ring
Though the dogs did bark
the cats meowed
when the nights were dark
to play out late then was not allowed

The boys played soccer ball
with goal posts of caps and shirts
the girls played chase though some got hurt
folks knew their place

For the streets were not so noisy then
we skipped and ran
we hopped and chased when we were young
in our play space

We danced and played the cobbled streets
hard brick and stone beneath our feet.

Ray Wills

During these times I would spend hours talking to kids on the streets in the midst of houses being demolished and aware of all the white dust and horror of rats which were in abundance. Each week I would collect groups of children from their family homes and escort them to the Sunday school service at St Barnabus church, then return them all home safely later. All such trips I considered an essential part of the adventure playgrounds life. Margaret Selby the community worker who lived in Sandford road Moseley and worked for the Council of Churches was aware that this role of play worker was as she often said a way of life. It was demanding, hard work and yet was extremely rewarding. The play leader's role on the playground was not in fact to lead, despite the title, the play leader was more of an enabler, providing opportunities for children to become involved. As a member of the newly formed Midlands Play Association, as well as (A.P.W.A) the Adventure Playgrounds Workers Association and the (N.P.F.A) National Playing Fields Association play leaders group meetings at Playfield House London. I was well aware of the needs and issues in play work. The (N.P.FA) National Playing Fields Association regional officer for the Midlands at that time was Nick Balmforth. I often attended meetings of the Midlands Play Association held at the Handsworth adventure playground Birmingham. One of its first leaders was Dave Swingle. The Handsworth adventure playground was at that time going through a difficult period of vandalism on the playground site. Its new leader John Huff was trying hard to resolve it and visited me on numerous occasions.

However by 1969 they were experiencing many problems as a result of racial tension and by the autumn of 1969 The Handsworth playground was also in severe financial difficulties. The actress Vanessa Redgrave had read about their plight and she came to Handsworth and was impressed by the playground and the local residents who helped to run it. She declared that she would raise big money by filling the Royal Albert Hall in London. She persuaded Ravi Shankar and Yehudi Menuhin to play at this fund raising event. Both had previously performed at the United Nations event for human rights but were also ready to support the playground. The hall was nearly full on the night. Ravi played his sitar, chatted to the audience and lost track of time – he had to rush away for a plane before he could speak. Thanks to Ravi, and the performers the playground was saved.

We were experiencing much smaller problems at The Balsall heath Malvern street Venture playground compared to Handsworth. Our playgrounds wooden slat fence was easily stripped by local vandals, or those intent on breaking in to the playground at night. It was becoming a problem especially when huge gaps were appearing everywhere. Despite us replacing the wood this continued to happen. Speaking with the children it became obvious that they were not to blame as some children then told me an old lady with a pram was doing it. Yet at the time I found this explanation somewhat hard to believe. Then one winter's night I hid out in a side alley close to the playground and waited. Then I saw her old lady with a pram with a hammer in her hand she was stripping the wood from the fence and placing the strips in her pram. I moved cautiously towards her and asked her what she thought she was doing. She answered "I'm getting some firewood". I explained to her that this was the kid's playground fence; she seemed surprised and offered to return the wood. I took her address and assured her that I would arrange fresh supplies of firewood for her. So began the adventure playgrounds firewood services for pensioners. The playground kids would break up spare wood and sack up and then deliver to local pensioners on a regular basis during winter months. An idea that I had originally undertaken at Redditch holiday play scheme. News at that time was of the death of a local mum from old balsall heath who suffered from a brain haemorrhage brought on by her damp housing living conditions. Shortly after a national daily newspaper The Daily Express did a featured story about her family and paid for her daughter to spend a day in London. Betty was fitted out in new clothes and the family were to have a perfect Xmas.

It was whilst attending the in service youth training course at Bourneville College under the direction of Howard Squires of Birmingham Youth Service that I met Revd David Collier. David at that time operated a youth club in his church hall in Wolverhampton which was called "The Double Zero". The church altar there was made from motorbike parts, for David was a bike enthusiast, his club was attended by the local chapter of greaser lads or hells angels. I recall seeing them at the church hall

all with their leather clothes and long hair, All swinging on the ropes which hung from the ceiling and throwing buckets of water at one another to let off steam. These Hells Angels ran an emergency blood transfusion service for the local hospital.

One evening when I was leading the youth club at the local church of Christ hall in Moseley road, I was aware that one of the youths (Billy) was a long time in the toilets. We discovered him in the process of removing the lead from the church roof. As the lad was already on probation the vicar and I made an arrangement to help him if he was agreeable. The lad became a regular helper at the youth club and the adventure playground. Such stories were common place whilst I was in Balsall Heath. A common reminder of the mixed cultures and the need to find alternative avenues for these young people. The playground was now attracting lots of children from a wider area including Sparkbrook and old Balsall heath, as a result of my detached work and visits to schools. On one occasion I was invited to the Shirley district of Birmingham to visit the girls comprehensive school to give a talk to senior pupils. The following evening I bumped into them again at a local fairground whilst I was escorting a young lady friend on the bumping cars. This was soon to become major big news amongst the girls at the school.

The ideal play leader was someone who embraced the work as a way of life. "Demanding an almost limitless talent for human relationships, judgment, perception administrative ability, a good and respected character and enormous physical toughness and stamina." The emphasis was on the individual's personal qualities rather than qualifications that made them technicians in playground management. It was little wonder that "burn out" was frequent; with the average working life of a play leader in this period being estimated as six to nine months.

Brian Shaw a close friend and voluntary assistant at the playground become a play leader of The Triangle Adventure playground in Kennington London. I was invited to visit him during this time and on my visit we went together to see the new production of the musical "Hair" at the Shaftesbury theatre in

London. I spent many happy times with Brian at the Triangle with its high tower with a view into the Oval cricket ground. At one time bringing my kid sister Diane along with me joining in the activities on the site.

The proprietors of the Clifton Public House in Clifton road were extremely helpful as a source in raising much needed playground funds with raffles and collections, or donations of crisps and pop. One of their young sons Norman Hassan was in later decade to become a founder member of the famous pop group UB40. A cheeky little half English, half Arab kid who was a close friend of Eugene Donnelly and who is still with the group today, he was always attending the adventure playground in those days. Along with all the other young people who had a strong desire to be actively involved in the running of the playground. My relationships with the youth of the area had a strong impact on the adventure playgrounds success. on the streets, in the youth clubs or in my visits to their family homes. From all their playground projects whether construction of elaborate dens or forts, one could see their comradeship with their peers develop both between their gang and with others. Whether sharing materials, resources, swopping or trading, sharing tools or with physical assistance in projects. There was also the creativity involved; whereby individuals and teams become more imaginative and skilled with tools. Creating ladders, ramps, doors, windows, hatches, fireplaces and brick chimneys. In such ways the adventure playground became a practical learning and educational resource. It thrived with ingenuity and creativeness, it was enriched and unique. The sense of worth, self esteem felt within individuals and its members spread throughout the scheme. "Something very special was happening here". Joy Henry a small dark skinned pretty Indian girl who was a regular on the Venture lived next door to me when I stayed with the Warren family in Clifton road. Joy lived with her mum Pat, her step dad, her younger sister and her step brother John Poutney and in the summer I arranged to take Joy with me on my vacation to Dorset. It was the first time she had been out of Balsall heath so it was quite a big adventure for her to travel on a coach to the countryside. Once we arrived in Bovington she was spoilt rotten by my family and had her very first bath in a real bath full of bubbles and it was obvious that she didn't want to come out.

When I returned to Birmingham and to the playground following my break during the hot summer sunshine. Tiny tots came to the Venture adventure playground with buckets and spades. To dig in the sandy play mounds (which we had intentionally constructed for this purpose), or assist their elders/peers with the building of the play dens. Many small girls decorated the little wooden houses which were appearing around the site daily with curtains and carpets. This all added variety to the assortment of dens which were now springing up all over the site. Little Indian girls came in groups, shy and hesitant. Pretty in their colourful summer outfits, playing games of skipping, holding hands or standing close to me for protection. Occasionally one would hear the sound of the noisy railway traffic which ran along the nearby bank facing the site. Carrying cars from the factories to the show rooms. On the other side of the railway bank was the industrial estate with its ice fruit pops factory. A treat which the kids loved during the hot weather and most popular sweet. I was aware that a great many of these iced pops were actually being stole or nicked by the children, though it couldn't be proven, probably had happened for years previously and a common practice. Throughout the summer months and well into the autumn the site buzzed with activity. One day I noticed children had a kind of rash so I called out the council health inspector who told me it was impetigo, an infection caused by the dust from the demolition. Through my street work I met up with many groups of lads who played ad hoc football on any vacant land. Forming a local league of teams from the neighbourhood, before I managed a local Asian football team known as the Hertford explorers. These lads aged from 11 to 14 years of age were extremely talented. Asian boys like Mukara Khan, Jazzbear Singh, Shar Singh, Mann Singh, Talah Mohad and Vipar Komar. They played football on the side streets or wastelands of Hertford and Malvern road, close to the adventure playground. One way in which the Association attempted to resolve the problem of break ins to the site at that time was to be tried out. That summer the army was invited to assist and a few soldiers came to the site to bolt together the playgrounds fencing. However they came the worse for drink as the local Clifton pub was more of an attraction. to them and we had to dismiss them. One evening after all the youth had spent many hours over weeks building a tall wooden tower climbing frame with walkways trap doors, fireplace and chimney and were proud of it. However, it was hurtful to see it completely demolished by the following morning. It could only have been dismantled overnight by adult regulars of the pub. During the days on the site we held regular camp building contests with prizes for best built dens. During the summer months the adventure playground resounded with the sounds of children hammering and sawing right into the evenings, creating a vast number of dens and small wooden boxed miniature houses.

Balsall Heath adventure playgrounds next leader was Robert Wheway. who was well known in Birmingham for organising the Sparkbrook Festival. Rob was to stay at the playground for a further 5 years until he was to become regional Midlands play officer for the N.P.F.A . By the time I had left Balsall Heath (1971) the adventure playground had its own permanent (Banbury buildings) play hut on site and operational. Two of my playground voluntary assistants at Balsall heath, Brian Shaw and Mike Halward, become adventure playground leaders in their own right in later years at the Triangle adventure playground London and Berkshire playgrounds. Mike eventually becoming a (N.P.F.A) National Playing Fields Association Play Officer in later years. Many others play workers were employed at Malvern street over the years. In 1976/ 1977 onwards these included Dave Swingle,Sheila Rushforth and Chris Leach.

Memories of the venture adventure playground from once former children of the area.

" I remember going there in the early 70s it was all cowboys and Indians stuff." " I think they had a jail if you were naughty or that was the threat anyway, and as I remember you could change your money for theirs. It was beside the railway line which you had to climb the embankment to reach".

"It must have been fairly famous at the time cos our mother brought us all the way from small heath to it".

"We had pretend money and cowboy hats and I am sure little camp fires it was brilliant for us kids" .

Kevin Lane - "Remember it well Holes in the dirt,lino to make slides,airial runways. A great place to be as a child with practically no H and S ."

Kate Donnelly - "I loved that place so much.Have the best memories of childhood there."

Marie Smith - "My Dad Joe Glenhomes was very involved in the Venture when it was actually set up".

I left the Balsall heath adventure playground in Malvern street in the knowledge that "the Venture" had become a reality. I was destined to establish adventure playgrounds in other communities elsewhere. So that by the time I left the Venture I knew most of the kids of the neighbourhood and a great many of their parents as friends. What a grand venture it had been.

Old Streets of Cobbled Stone.
I chased that childhood laughter
down streets of cobbled stones
 where dogs were barking daily
 where no strangers walked alone

 I watched the joy at daybreak
 the sighs of mothers all
 the shouts of merriment at play
 the joy of childhoods call

 I heard the thrill of fun and games
 the spinning of the tops
 the skipper's of the rope's that spun

the little Goldilocks

The boys at footy games and cheers
 when they scored within their posts
 of coats and jumpers scattered there
 afore they all eloped

For love was born in poverty
 where charity was mourned
 when children played at kiss and chase
 with shoes so old and worn

Down dusty streets they played each day
 then beneath the lamp at night
 where moon and stars they shone so bright
 upon their old community so sprite

When Brummy boys and Brummy gals
 were playing happily.

Ray Wills

CHAPTER SEVEN

ROGERSTONE LOG CABIN

Rogerstone log cabin play centre

In the valley

Its peaceful in the valley
  where the lambs and rabbits play
  where the linnets build their nests
  just half a mile away

  where the wind Berry's are growing
  on the banks and heathered down
  where the sun shines in the mornings
  just as the moon goes down

The deer runs in the woodlands
  the hills are green and thick

there's farming in the valleys still
along with Dylan Thomas- Dai and rick

Here the history tells of miners
working down the pits
when the children died in Aberavan
where kids still respect their mum

There's singers of great stature
grand choirs throughout this fair land
in a world of peace and beauty
let me take your hand

Il show you the hills of Brecon
with the streams all running free
the lovely Abergavenny
Wales is so beautiful to me

Its peaceful in the valley
where the lambs and rabbits play
where the linnets build their nests
just half a mile away.

Ray Wills

Following my success in establishing Balsall Heath adventure playground in Birmingham I attended three interviews for positions in play. I was offered all of these posts and had to make the decision of which one to accept. These included Hill-fields play centre in Coventry which was a local education department project, Mint Street adventure playground in Southwark London site of former children's workhouse which Dickens used for his story Oliver Twist. The other was for the new log cabin play centre at Rogerstone village in Gwent South Wales. This was a joint project for Rogerstone Parish Council and Magor and St Melons Rural District Council. After much thought and reflection I chose to accept the Rogerstone log cabin play centre post.

The Rogerstone project in Gwent where I now worked was in complete contrast to the Balsall Heath community in Birmingham. Here there were few busy roads, little heavy traffic and no slums. Rogerstone was a welsh village with a mixture of housing old and new, council and private. A great deal of the landscape was un spoilt, quiet and tranquil with scenic beauty of fields, the Cefn woodlands and the Brecon beacon hills in the distance. The play centre site was within fields next to the Cefn woods and situated in a basin overlooked by the hills of the Brecon beacons and the High Cross pre war red bricked housing estate and recreation grounds. Alongside the site were modern built family housing units and senior citizen bungalow dwellings. In the far distance was the local parish village with its church, school and cricket grounds. he play centre was a new log cabin which had been imported from Norway. On my first visit to Rogerstone I took the bus from Newport to High cross. I then strolled down the steep hill to the play centre cabin site in the basin of the valley below. It was a beautiful sunny day, a Sunday, I was aware of a large group of Sunday school children from the local chapel on the hill, playing noisy chase games on the green grassy recreation area. Then I became aware of the panoramic view of the valley below and the surrounding green meadows and far in the distance the view of the Brecon Hills. I was taken aback by the freshness and the beauty of the landscape stretched out below. A remarkable contrast when compared to the harshness of the Birmingham city, Balsall heath I had left behind with its busy roads and high density housing. The plush green fields of Rogerstone and the panoramic view up to the hill of Abergavenny and beyond were a great attraction to visitors from the cities. In the days that were to follow I would regularly be up here on this same area of wide sloping green recreational expanse. Often accompanied by hordes of children from the neighbourhood. Playing games of "pond and bank" and "stuck in the mud" along with the traditional "oranges and lemons". Or along with the older boys playing ad hoc games of soccer using coats and jumpers as goal posts. Therefore before starting work in the play centre I had chosen to work in the community as a detached worker on the estate. In this way I felt I would be best able to operate the new project after I had built up solid relationships with the local young people. I worked on the streets, playing fields and in the local youth clubs. Whilst at the same time building contacts and resources with community leaders. I felt this was the right way to operate prior to officially opening the play centre log cabin. Therefore by the time I was ready I had built a strong relationship with local youngsters.

LOG CABIN

Once a had a log cabin
sheltered in the sun
it lie in south Wales valley
where children all did run

There were fields of open meadow
hills of scenic views
in a village they called Rogey
many miles from Poole

Hundreds of kids played there
in the little cabin home
there were birds in the woodlands
squirrels that never roamed
a was the kids play leader
south Wales was my home

In the little Norwegian cabin
we played games of fun n chase
with lots of balls n bats
where folks they knew their place

The little log cabin
with scenic views

the hills of abergavinny
at night the stars shone through

The grass there was green n rich
the sky was oh so blue
in the little hillside valley
many miles from Poole.

Ray Wills

My first summer on the play centre site was exhilarating and exhausting. A period full of events for the local children flocked to the cabin in their hundreds. They took part in a wide programme of events and activities, including art work sessions, table tennis tournaments, recreational games and sports. We were able to make full use of the large expanse acreage of recreational space on the estate as well as in the nearby Cefn woodlands for adventurous pursuits. So many children attended that we had to extend the scheme to the village playing fields also, such was the demand. The Magor and St Melons Council employed extra temporary play assistants for the summer period to help me cope. We made good use of the Cefn woodland area for mass games of chase, run out and here large aerial runways and Tarzan swings were also created. I was like an adventure play park with tire swings and giant commando nets. All of this was a great attraction to the children of Rogerstone and hordes of children of all ages used all these resources daily throughout the hot summer. When the kids played in the Cefn woodlands their favourite traditional game was called run out, a game that was very energetic and could last for hours. We would often play this within the deep woodland ferns and bushes situated at the edge of the cabin. Often hundreds of kids and youths were involved in this activity. Mike Guy one of the regulars fell from one of the woodland runways and had to go to hospital.

The play centre also focused on the social problem kids of the area, many of these were well hidden until now. By now I had a temporary assistant play leader appointed, my friend Mike Halward who had originally assisted me at Balsall Heath adventure

102

playground in Birmingham. We would regularly organise a large number of day trips and excursions to places like Newport adventure playground. Here we worked alongside the vibrant, fit and attractive leggy blonde Helen Gush, leader of the Newport site. The Newport adventure playground ran alongside the railway line and to the rear of the large council housing estate with its own recreation grounds and large natural pond. Here we took part in inter playground competitions as well as inviting them to the Rogerstone play centre on a regular basis. It was at one of these activities in Newport that I slipped fell and broke my arm whilst playing soccer. My arm was set in a cast and of course all the kids wanted to put their signatures on it and soon I had a cast packed with literally loads of names. When I visited Playfield House later the N.P.F.A persuaded me to donate them the autographed cast which they displayed in a glass case. The problems of the Newport adventure playground were many. It was at one stage arsoned and all burnt to the ground. A child attendee was blinded by a dart and vandalism and break ins on the site was common practice. However, despite all this the popular Helen Gush persevered, gaining much local community support from her loyal band of helpers. Often she would visit me at Rogerstone. When Helen later left her adventure playground and married a probation officer in London. On her last day there the kids threw her fully clothed into the nearby pond as a final farewell gesture it was there way of saying thanks.

At Rogerstone log cabin many tiny tots were attending the project till late at night up until the darker autumn evenings. I voiced my concerns at this at a local council meeting which was unfortunately taken up by the Cardiff Times which published a front page article entitled, "Playgroup leader slams Parents". Later I had to explain this to the local parents who in the vast majority supported my concerns and stance. Following this a great many small children were then collected from the site in the evenings by older brothers and sisters. Shortly after a group of local parents showed great interest in forming a parents group to fund raise and organise activities. I was therefore able to organize a public open evening from which a parents association evolved. The Rogerstone youths sported long hair, wore flared trousers and Dr Martin boots, were as, in nearby Cardiff city the youths were skinheads and dressed in jeans and bracers. These two groups skinheads and Grebos were often involved in fights in Newport. The local lads were terrified of being confronted by the Cardiff skins who rumour had it travelled the estates in cars looking for them. Newport town centre at weekends was often a no go area for local lads when the skins visited the town. The youths in attendance at the cabin grew in numbers and requested a youth section. Discussions followed with the council officers and members of the county council and it was approved that we could operate later in the evenings for this group. This newly formed section began their activities with regular weekly discos with music provided by a club member Gary Rogers.

Other successful events were to follow these included a Senior Citizens Evening supervised by the youth section. This event included a chicken salad meal for the pensioners with music of old-time favourites played by a local beat group. The local Probation Officer was invited to attend regularly and became involved in many of the cabins activities. On one occasions supporting me in a venture to escort a youth group on an overnight expedition across and over the Brecon Beacons which was the major landscape in the terrain and it raised funds to finance the pensioners evenings. Karen a small lively child and play centre regular wrote to the (N.P.F.A)National Playing Fields about the log cabin and her letter was printed in their glossy play publication monthly magazine "Play Right". One of the young girls using the centre Helen Kent daughter of Mrs Josie Kent. Helen taught me a lot of the children's playground rhymes. This is one which is a bit saucy.

UNDER THE BRAMBLES

Under the brambles down by the leas
true love to you my darling true love to me
then when were married wel raise a family
a boy for you a girl for me
that's the way that it will be
be bom be bom Esso blue.

It was obvious that the Log Cabin venture could not be fully developed as an adventure playground because of its close proximity to senior citizens housing and there were to be no building of dens or play structures here. This was due also to local peoples concept as child's play being a noisy and unsightly activity. The Log Cabin however did focus well on the local concerns of the area, which until then were usually hidden. Unfortunately besides the holiday periods the cabin was not adequately staffed to cater for the increasing demands and numbers of the children in attendance. Despite my constant demands for increased supervision. I had to rely on youth members assistance with the Guy brothers attending regularly. At one time Michael Guy taking over the reins of the cabin for a short period. The Log Cabin building itself was of solid pine log structure but it lacked the most necessary fittings for its windows, pipes and guttering were all plastic. An open invitation to wear and tear and vandalism. Each morning I would walk small children from their homes on the red bricked council estate and down the steep grassy hill to open up the cabin, in the valley below. Constantly picking up gathering hordes of small children on the route. Many of them heard the jingly sounds of my small bells which I wore on the bottom rim of my fashionable bell bottom green flared corduroy trousers and the youths called me tinker bell lol. Many of the children at the Cabin painted pictures and crayoned masterpieces daily. The youths at the cabin were very helpful and supportive and also were very good with the small kids as very good voluntary assistants. One of the play centre youth members wanted to know more about play and attended the (N.P.F.A) National Playing Fields Association Play leadership course at Kennington College with me on a regular basis. The course was run by the Inner London Education Authority and (LAPA) London Adventure Playground Association. Its tutors were Alan Curtis from (N.P.F.A) National Playing Fields Association and Virginia Bottomley of The Child Poverty Action Group. Virginia remarked," that with the pressure of space, the facility which can be used by the largest numbers of children for physical exercise in the smallest space is the Adventure Playground". In later years Virginia was to enter politics and became a conservative M.P. Often I would travel to attend numerous play related local, regional and national conferences or meetings with other play people. Often these were organised by N.P.F.A. who were always kept up to date with my progress at Rogerstone. During this time I attended the official opening of the national sports centre at Cardiff meeting up once again with Drummond Abernethy of (N.P.F.A.)National Playing Fields Association. Attending meetings with local council play officers and councilors at Central Hall at Westminster in London. I also with Jim Jackson, Pat Smythe, Mike Buckley, Francis Mc Lennon and others attended the first meeting of the newly formed (APWA) Adventure Play Workers Association at Notting Hill adventure playground in London. At one of the regular Play Workers meetings at (N.P.F.A s) National Playing Fields Associations Playfield House London play worker Sue Townsend said her final farewells to Drummond and us all. As she was leaving adventure play to concentrate on writing her very successful children's books. The (NPFA) National Playing Fields Association now had a team of seven Regional Officers previous adventure play workers supporting their role to establish the standards for adventure playgrounds. During these years Drummond Abernethy of the (N.P.F.A) National Playing Fields Association was travelling around the U.K giving talks to communities and local councils on the importance of providing adventure playgrounds. As well as promoting the idea that "Special pavilions needed to be built in parks for children. That recreation grounds should be within half a mile radius from a child home and that schools and other provisions should open during the evening, weekends and during school holidays. By 1971 the (NPFA) National Playing Fields Association had employed a team of seven Regional Officers who were all previous adventure playground leaders. All supporting the NPFA's role to establish the standards for adventure playgrounds. The N.P.F.A provided some short training courses operated from Playfield house and in time many colleges like Kennington and Goldsmiths were persuaded to provide part time training play leadership courses'.

Because of social problems in the Rogerstone village, mainly due to kids playing too close to houses, I was instructed to help out.

I agreed to collect children daily from across the village and bring them across to the site through the winding riverside track and I was helped by the elder youths from the cabin Mike and Martin Guy with this project. This was quite a walk away from the Cabin centre. During the autumn months we had organized a community bonfire and fireworks display. This attracted hundreds of participants. We had our very own St John's Ambulance officer in David Jones a play centre member. This was a most successful venture with a guy Fawkes competition and fireworks supervised by the youth section. In the winter the Welsh Rugby team were stranded overnight and had no where to stay. They were sent to me by the local chapel leader for help and I hurriedly made the necessary arrangements for them to sleep overnight at the cabin. The play centre kids thought this was really amazing. They were collecting autographs from all their favorite players before the cabin closed for the day.

The nearby village post office was the greatest source for local gossip and if you wanted to know anything you would find it out there. Because of my long hair and appearance, flared trouser, Beatle boots and English accent I was thereby branded as a Hippy. Along with the fact that I would lay out on the grass and relax prior to starting work each day at the cabin. Thus I was seen as a Hippy employed by the council, encouraging delinquency by mixing with the youth of the area. There was even a rumour going the rounds that I was taking kids to the pub on High Cross. The log cabin had lots of successful enterprises with hundreds of kids involved daily throughout the year. In the holidays I found myself coordinating the full programme at the cabin, plus the youth section. As well as a holiday play scheme locally and others in the Rogerstone village. Out of the success of the Senior Citizens party a Senior Citizens group was established at the cabin. Discussions were also taking part with the council to operate a children's Nursery, or preschool playgroup at the cabin in the mornings and a public meeting took place in the Cabin. We entered the local carnival with two floats created by our busy parents group. One of the mums ran a dressmaking shop in Newport and many of our log cabin parents such as Mrs Guy and Mrs Margaret Jones were involved in making costumes for the kids over many weeks. It was all well worth it when we won first prize at the Rogerstone carnival with our float "Indian Reservation". The children wore real authentic looking war paint and those fabulous costumes and looked fabulous.

Village Children.
We were the village children
lost to reels of rhyme
we were stranded in our imaginations
lost in another place and time

We were the village children
just let out to play
we wallowed in our innocence
trapped in this moment today

We were the village children
destined t impart
our dreams and fantasies of love
like a candle wick just sparked

We were the village children
all grown old in time
lost our hopes and innocence
planted on the vine.

Ray Wills

The log cabins youth section went from strength to strength. One of its members Haydn Berry won the Gwent county table tennis championship. Relationships with the parents of children remained sound. I had now a nucleus of supporters and I was regularly invited to speak at local schools on the value of Child's play. Winter periods at the cabin were obviously not so busy and attendances fell due to colder darker evenings. However, indoor activities continued and appeared to be just as popular amongst the regulars. There were regular disco evenings, parents evenings, table tennis competitions, crazy games of indoor five a side football. Art and Craft sessions continued to be popular, these were well supervised by Mrs Insley and Moira Kent The parents association became very proactive, pressing the council for an improved bus service and footpaths to the village. (Which for most of the year was waterlogged due to the subway being usually flooded).The youth section organized an evening disco for the tiny tots, this event was called a Teeny Boppers Disco and went down a treat with everyone. The younger children came in droves on the evening, all dressed up with their modern trendy party clothes, little handbags and wearing their mums make up. The event was a brilliant success, which the youths had really enjoyed organizing, it was such a joy just to see the kids pleasure on the day. During my annual holiday i took a boy from the centre Christopher Pritchard away with me to Dorset which he still can recall in great detail.

The local education welfare officer was also the pub landlord at the Rogey Hotel in the village and he was very supportive throughout and believed in the concept of child's play. During my second winter at the cabin, I had an accident playing five a side football with the exuberant youth in the cabin and broke my leg. I had therefore to rest for weeks and had to close up the cabin having no other paid staff available to take over.(Despite my pleas for temporary assistants).During these weeks the cabin was broken into on a number of occasions, although no real damage was committed and detergent was scattered around. I was instructed by the council to patrol the grounds on a regular basis each evening. But instructed not to open up, as a punishment to the children for the break ins. It was around this time that my friend Mike Halward who had assisted me in Birmingham visited and was appointed as assistant play leader for the school holidays. Unfortunately Mike was attacked by a troubled youth and now sported a black eye. Mike was great at scrounging play materials from the local factories for kids play use and excellent with the young children and popular with parents. Mike in later years went on to operate his own play schemes, adventure playgrounds and as regional (N.P.F.A) National Playing Fields

Association Officer. By the time the log cabin was reopened the council had appointed a new leader. The guy they appointed was a part time prison officer from Cardiff Prison and he turned up with an Alsatian dog on a chain. "Talk about over reacting". He was to oversee the youth section in a senior role to me and his role was to "discipline" the youth of the area. As a direct result of the councils new policy, numbers of youth attending fell dramatically, it changed from a youth facility to a physical culture club. As the guy had them doing physical jerks. Since my appointment I had lodged with a family on the estate, however now even this was to come to an abrupt end. An official from the housing department visited the family and said that the house was overcrowded and that consequently I would have to find alternative accommodation. Fortunately the family who lived in their own house on the opposite side of the road took me in as their lodger. It was then I met Dana the famous Irish pop singer who had won the Euro-vision song contest. Dana stayed with the family at weekends, her father was a close friend of theirs. I can truthfully say I gave up my room and bed for her and slept on the sofa. the family had two small boys who came to the cabin each day, they would always be close to me. During those weeks the local parents got up a petition in support of me and many signed. I was not happy with the strain the local council had put on me and approached both the (N.P.F.A) National Playing Fields Association and (APWA) Adventure Playground Workers Association in London for advice. However there was little they could do apart from listen and support me. Around this time I attended the opening of the new Sports centre in Cardiff which was part of a national IPA play conference event.

Cardiff operated two adventure playgrounds in the city both of which were organized through Cardiff Voluntary Community Services and were extremely successful.

I had arranged to meet up with Drummond at the Cardiff conference and I introduced Mrs Insley to him and later he gave his talk on Child's play to a packed audience. Drummond would give instances from the bible and Greek history concerning the problems of unsociable children in early societies showing that these were not new problems just of our present community.

During this time I occasionally visited play leaders at the Bristol adventure playgrounds. Adventure playgrounds were operating then at St Paul's, Easton Lockleaze, Southmead and Windmill Hill.

Jim Jackson told my story of the problems that I was experiencing at Rogerstone in the (APWA) Adventure Playground Workers Association newsletter at the time . Alan Curtis Drummond's Assistant and the former writer of "The Pen" counselled me. However by then I had decided that I would leave the log cabin centre voluntary rather than be pushed, or dismissed by the parish council in an awkward situation where I felt victimized. The Rogerstone situation had taught me a lot, politics was dirty, where play work was new and invigorating, obviously some people felt threatened by new ideas like local democracy. Some areas of the U.K were obviously not yet ready for local participation in decision making. It was a case where power was in the hands of people who were fearful of involving local people in their community.

I will always remember the success of the parents organization at the cabin. Their organization of the winning float at the carnival procession," Indian reservation", created by Mrs Guy and Mrs Jones. Along with the exuberant youths Mike and Martin Guy and gang with the regular five a side soccer games in the cabin. The success of the youths teeny boppers disco, the senior citizens group and the trips to my friend Helen Gush's Newport adventure playground. The thrill of the fireworks at the bonfire and fireworks event and David member of the Youth Section in his St John's Ambulance outfit as first aid officer on the night. But beyond all this the fond memories I recall of hordes of children of all ages walking alongside me each day enjoying their play times in such a beautiful setting. The Rogerstone experience had taught me many lessons along with providing me with many fresh ideas and inspirations for new adventure playgrounds in the future. It had also taught me new skills in community involvement, which I would be able to put to good use in the future.

I returned to Rogerstone in 2004,(over 30 year later) whilst I was attending a Bob Dylan concert in Cardiff. I was to be amazed at the changes in the area. No longer was there any sign of a log cabin, or fields, or scenic view of the Brecon hills from the valley, for the whole area had changed dramatically. Now there was just large private housing development and private mansions everywhere. I found it difficult to find any of the old landmarks I had previously known so well, or see any of the people I had previously known as children. The Rogerstone Hotel in the village was now an Indian restaurant, the underpass was gone, now there was a motorway and a flyover passing through the landscape. Whilst the former village school was empty, bordered up and used as a storehouse. However I still had my memories of the plush green meadows, sloping fields, a chapel on a hillside, hordes of happy Welsh kids at play and noisy exuberant youth. And a Norwegian log cabin situated in a valley surrounded by a beautiful landscape and the sounds of the Cefn woodlands bird song, echoing across the terrain.

Early in 1972 I took up the temporary post of play scheme leader at Walpole road Boscombe for Bournemouth Borough Councils Parks Department. The first of its kind in the Borough. Based at Walpole road Boscombe with the recreation officers Roger Browne's wife Janet Browne as my assistant. This scheme proved a big success and through it I established the Walpole road Play Association which went on to operate a number of schemes and parties for local children in the area for a number of years after.

CHAPTER EIGHT

THE PIN GREEN ADVENTURE PLAYGROUND – STEVENAGE.

Adventure playground children Stevenage

Stevenage in Hertfordshire was the very first of the constructed New Towns of Britain, primarily built to house post-war Londoners. The Town Centre in Stevenage was revolutionary, with the very first pedestrian shopping centre in the country. It drew in visitors from several of the surrounding towns to do their shopping in style. The establishment of new community adventure playgrounds, at Stevenage was to become the forerunner of the play movement in the years ahead. Adventure playgrounds sprung up in Stevenage; mainly as a result of the pioneering work of individual adventure play leaders like Donne Buck, one of its founding fathers.

Donne Buck was the first play worker at Stevenage and was based at the Bandley Hill Adventure Playground Stevenage from 28th March 1967 - 6th June 1971. At this time he also joined the International Play Association, another of Lady Allen's innovations. This brought him into contact with a vast family of other play workers in the UK and throughout the world.

Donne Buck-" My salary was funded from the shilling a week lottery by the time I arrived in Stevenage they had about a thousand pounds in the bank, which was enough to pay my salary for a year plus some of the overheads. " ."I can't remember exactly how it was funded. My salary was funded from the shilling a week lottery by the time I arrived in Stevenage they had about a thousand pounds in the bank, which was enough to pay my salary for a year plus some of the overheads; electricity and water and that sort of thing, but only just. And so, knowing what a tremendous effort local people were putting into the funding of the playground, and into other aspects of voluntary work, running the committee and so on, I gradually managed to get into fundraising myself for the playground and eventually set up a market stall in the local shopping area, mainly selling jumble with help from some of the parents and towards the end of my time there I was able to raise enough money for a sort of petty cash side of things, to not have to call on the local committee for petty cash to fund the petrol for the van and nails and tools and that sort of thing, for the children, paint and paper and brushes and all of that sort of thing for the artwork, I was able to cover most of that from the money I raised myself". The (NPFA) National Playing Fields Association often sent local council groups and officers to Stevenage to see Donne Buck at Bandley Hill Adventure Playground. From Donne they were to best learn how play could be developed and this practice was to continue during my years there. Donne's pioneering work in Stevenage resulted in the development of a chain of adventure playgrounds in the New Town. It also resulted in an invitation to join the staff of the newly formed Peterborough Development Corporation's Social Development Department as their Children's Play Officer.

Stevenage was to operate a variety of such playgrounds and centres throughout the new town. All of these were neighbourhood based, at Bandley Hill, Chells, Canyon, Pin Green and at St Nicholas and all were to become outstanding examples of community adventure play areas. All were managed by local play associations and all came under the umbrella of and part of the Stevenage Play Association. Which in later years was to become "The Stevenage Play Council". The Stevenage Play Association received a separate operational grant from the Stevenage Borough Council; this covered training courses, play functions and social events. When I came to Stevenage I first lodged with Dorothy the playgrounds secretaries home and then for a while with June Watson play leader at Hampson scheme. Before eventually moving to live in a guest house in Stevenage old town, run by Ray Guest and his wife who later moved to live in sunny Bournemouth to manage a hotel by the sea. I loved the Stevenage old town with its low beamed tea shop Tudor cafe and its famous Cromwell pub. Where was filmed "Here We Go Round the Mulberry Bush". I would often take Sue Riley for a coffee in the Tudor tea shop cafe, or arrange to meet my friend Joy Walton there. Stevenage was also the location for the famous film "Billy Liar".

I was initially invited to apply for the Pin Green adventure playgrounds leader position and I met up with an old friend Jim Jackson there , who was now the newly appointed Social

Development Officer for the Stevenage Development Corporation. I had known Jim since he was a play leader at Telford and we had both attended the play leaders meetings in NPFA Playfield House and at Notting Hill Adventure Playground in the days when he was chairman of the Adventure Playground Workers Association in the late 1960s. Mike Fowler play leader based at Bandley Hill Adventure Playground originally told me about the vacant position at Pin Green Stevenage. When I had a pint with him in St James Park London close to N.P.F.A s Playfield House after we had both attended a play leaders meeting there. Jim Jackson also encouraged me to apply for the Stevenage post following my ordeal at Rogerstone. Shortly after I applied for the post and was later interviewed in the play hut at Pin Green adventure playground by members of the Pin Green Play Association including its chairman David Kershaw and Donne Buck leader of the Bandley Hill adventure playground. Jim Jackson soon became a regular visitor to Pin Green Adventure Playground after my appointment.

Pauline at the entrance to playground on the opening day

The Pin Green adventure playground site was situated within the grounds of the hampson park. Almost surrounded by playing fields, a copse and car park and nearby was the Hampson pavilion and children's hard surface swing park. The playground had only been in operation for a few years then and was to some extent in need of practical work. Andy a former playground user at pin green had been acting alone as the play leader and needed help, as there had not been any trained leadership for quite a while. Despite this Andy had maintained much enthusiasm for the playground amongst its users and he had built up a big following particularly amongst local youths. He showed a keen interest in construction work of play towers, along with an interest in snooker, table tennis and pop music. Andy was easy going with a very pleasant manner, extremely popular and keen to assist me in the future playground development. Although the playground had its official opening in 1972 With Mrs Hampton being presented with a bouquet of flowers by local girl Pat Lancaster one of the playground regulars. On the day of my appointment in 1972 the local newspaper Stevenage Gazette ran a piece about me but concentrated on my years as a painter decorator rather than as a play leader. From the very first day of appointment I saw my main objective was to clear the site of rubble and weeds including nettles and brambles and to make it a safe place for children to play. The object being to project an image of safety and to be positive in a businesslike manner to encourage local children and their parents. I found the children were very receptive to this and eager to assist me. And so it was that within just a few days we had prepared the site for child's play to begin. At that time the site had few facilities to offer, although there was a sound brick play building built by local labour. With an activity room, an office, a kitchen, toilets and storage space. On the site there was an aerial runway, a pets area, a preschool play area, a play tower and a wooden tower made of palettes. Apart from these there were few facilities, most of the play activity stemmed from the play building. The play building itself was vitally important for indoor activities such as art and crafts, recreational, snooker, darts, cards or music with regular disco events and with a kitchen and the sales of refreshments, an essential aspect of the adventure playgrounds life. With community involvement and the organization of events and activities, both on site and in the wider community, trips out and special play events. An office with a telephone, filing system, along with first aid facilities, was essential. The adventure playground with regular attendance, following its official opening had to provide a full range of essential services, including toilets, washing and cooking facilities, electricity and water, along with sewerage services. Which all had to be brought into the playground site and into the building itself. Access to emergency services, such as fire and ambulance services, had to be catered for, with wide gate entrances and exits. Along with secure ground foundations for heavy vehicles, with sufficient room for turning of such large vehicles. The facilities both in the play building and outside in the playground itself, had to be accessible to all of its many users, whilst any additional facilities when required, had to be provided for. Such range of services could well include facilities for the disabled child, pre-school play areas, youth section, a garden, a pets area, music facilities, holiday play scheme, sports and others, required for the specific needs of groups or individual children. The job demands flexibility and a willingness to work unsociable hours as well as to be adaptable within a team setting. The leader has to be at ease with this style and discipline, within the chaos, the element of excitement and freedom of adventure there. The most successful people have been those who have possessed a healthy enthusiasm for the play vocation. Along with an endless pleasure in work with children a positive attitude, confidence in themselves and the philosophy of play work with leadership. Skills in construction, building work, carpentry, cooking, crafts, sports activities, games and first aid are all valuable assets. Specialist knowledge in such key areas as counselling, welfare or social work along with health and education including solvent abuse and drugs were also useful. Through the ability to scrounge a vast assortment and variety of play materials. To be proficient at organizing play events and activities both on and off the project in the wider community for all are essential attributes. The play leader has to have a good relationship with the parents of the children attending the project and there are countless opportunities to develop this important aspect of the job. There is no cut and dry rule to success as a play worker, it is true that mistakes were made in the past. With wrong decisions and numerous setbacks in the many efforts to develop and establish successful adventure playgrounds, as well as other schemes in play. Therefore, much of the special creative skills for the job depended on the particular chosen sites and neighbourhood support. Along with the many varied attributes of all involved in these demanding ventures. The job itself demanded an attitude of character rather than any particular discipline. So often, a positive vibrant personality was a blessing. However experienced or talented the play leader may be they will need to grow with the community and they with him or her. Apart from the most obvious aspects of the adventure playground leaders skills and responsibilities. Such as building sound relationships with and amongst the kids, providing a multitude of play opportunities and resources, other attributes were vital. These included their varied abilities to create play structures for the children to play on, as well as climbing for sliding down or running on, or other pursuits, such as skate boarding and bike riding. These facilities ranged from large and high walk- way towers, aerial runways, swings, slides, commando nets, and climbing frame structures. Construction undertaken by the playground staff and volunteers was an important day-to-day exercise, largely dependent upon their own individual and group construction skills. The job had so many dimensions from decorating the play structures to designing footpaths for use by the disabled children with their wheelchairs.

There was an active preschool playgroup on the playground ran by Mary Wake, which was an important integral part of the playground. There was also a local boy's football team, called "The Adventurers", who regularly used the building as a meeting place. The local neighbourhood policeman Peter Lynch was a member of the play committee, as was the probation officer Charles Watson. His wife June Watson operated the councils play scheme at the nearby Hampson park pavilion. Both the local bobby Peter Lynch and Charlie the probation officer, were regular playground visitors and were popular figures with the children. The playground management committee met monthly in the play building. Here all aspects of the playgrounds concerns were discussed. I gave my report here which included how the playground was doing with all our plans and programme of activities for the month ahead. Any specific problems which we were concerned about and the numbers using the site and needs for new equipment etc. The preschool playgroup leader gave her Report as well as the Treasurers Report. There were also regular play leaders meetings here as well as the annual play association meeting.

Georgina a bubbly thirteen year old regular at the playground told me about her accident on the playground aerial runway a year earlier, when she lost the top of her thumb. One of the very few playground accidents at pin green. That summer of 1972, was to be the most exciting and rewarding period in the playgrounds history. My day of work on the site covered a multitude of activities and tasks; these could include the following account. I would arrive on the site early each day to open up the padlocked main metal gates to the site and then open up the play hut building and prepare for the day ahead. Shortly after, the preschool playgroup staff would arrive and I would assist them in their preparations for the preschool children and stay and be involved in the sessions. Once the toddlers had left, I would inspect the playground and do a safety check of equipment on site and remove any discarded dangerous items. I would carry out any necessary repairs and phone up suppliers of materials. Often I would phone up other local play leaders to arrange a meeting, a function, or to talk over an issue. Often arrange to attend meetings on other playgrounds, or at pin green playground. By the mid afternoon I was prepared for the children, who came after schools had finished for the day. They queued up at the playground heavy iron gates ready for official opening time and I was fully prepared with supplies of tools, materials and nails on hand. Often these queues of children stretched to the nearby Hampson Park and included children of all ages. Many arrived on their push bikes, usually mountain bikes, there would be small kids holding hands of an older brother or sister and groups of youths talking. The ebb and flow of active kids coming and going, became an important aspect of the adventure playground. There was always something happening here, with new attractions, a fascination, or an event needing their attention. Kids moved freely from one activity, or interest, to another. So much depended upon the ability of the play leader and the efficiency and the co-operation of his playground management team. In many ways the adventure playground provided a miniature setting for all of life's happenings. A place where children could contribute to the whole, whether in the playgrounds construction, the community involvement, or local life with all of the associated happenings, risks, role playing, leisure, work and its full share of day to day playground comings and goings. It was to become a metropolis of activity where children shared in the common experience of play.

Andy my assistant and I worked on a number of projects at the site including the construction of a children's roundabout, which was an interesting venture. This roundabout was constructed from wood pallets, padded out with foam and carpets and situated on a revolving wheel and palette base, it was situated upon a high earth mound in the middle of the site. Once completed this project proved to be extremely successful, with hordes of children queuing up and using it constantly each day.

Compared to the roundabout in the local swing park, this facility was streets ahead in popularity and with a safe surface. Many of our activities at pin green were well supported with assistance from the councils park grounds man John ,who was based at Hampson Park. John would often mark out pitches on the playing fields, or support us with loans of equipment, such as an extended water hose for the barbecues, or future bonfires. A number of our youths would go across to help him with his work, so this was a good mutual understanding between Hampson Park and the playground. At one time there was trouble from children entering the playground when closed at night and this was overcome by the council planting special tall and wide bushes with protruding prickles around the perimeter of the playgrounds vertical concrete slat fencing.

We had a while ago obtained a noisy capstone siren from somewhere which was based in the office and we used this as a signal to open, or close the playground. The gates would then be unlocked and pushed wide open to ensure safe access for the rush, or stampede of kids or perhaps the regular delivery of timber supplies. Once in the site many children headed straight to their individual den, or project, whilst others went into the play hut. A few would look into the offices to see what was on the play programmed, or for details of the weeks future activities ahead. In the evenings the siren of the capstone would sound loud echoing across the Pin Green neighbourhood, heralding the playgrounds closing for the day. This was the signal for the return of tools and farewells between children and staff. Soon the playground became still and quiet.

As play leaders we floated between the activities in the hut and on the site. Ensuring that all was going well. Breaking up an occasional dispute, or manning the barbecue, or the play structures. Such was our role until the late evening, only broken by visits to the kitchen for refreshments, or to the office, to answer a phone call, or attend to first aid. Children would leave for tea and return later refreshed. The adventure playground had its own football team which was formed before I was appointed. Although they held their meetings in the play hut yet the soccer team members rarely used the playground. Members of the Stevenage play association mainly led by Les Lewis took it upon themselves to move a homeless family overnight into empty corporation housing and providing them with candles blankets and food until the electrical and gas supplies were turned on.

Jack Lambert was having great success at his adventure playground in Welwyn Garden City around this time as he wrote in his future splendid book. Adventure playgrounds. Jack Lambert -"I saw the opportunity of starting such a playground in an English New Town. Among the neat, ordered rows of front gardens with their rosebushes and little lawns there were a small number of children who rebelled against the hire-purchase-washing-machine culture with unfortunate results for the rosebushes. Surely if their energies could be channelled in the right setting, i.e. a play- ground without adults. With gardens rosebushes where they could dig and splash and build and make bonfires to their heart's content, the parents would be able to cultivate their gardens in peace and the children would be happy? It took a year's hard work by a small band of enthusiasts to explain the idea of the playground, negotiate with the authorities, collect money from those who were willing to give, scout out tools from remote surplus stores, and find a playground leader, a site, scrap materials, get lava- tones built, fencing and a hut. The support of Lady Allen of Hurtwood (who charmed us all when she came to give a lecture to the Community Association), as well as that of the National Playing Fields Association was a great help". "The children flocked in, and the site, which was rough grassland, in a short while looked like a peace field battlefield; earth dug up enthuse elastically, houses built (the best of them by a gang with the reputation for smashing lamp-standards); potatoes roasted on bonfires; and they came back again and again. It was difficult to gauge local reactions- there were pictures and reports in the local press, polite and very mildly appreciative. But also "cartoons" depicting vicious behaviour and vandalism. (One child in fact did start to hack the bark off a venerable tree. The explanation that this would kill the tree satisfied him sufficiently to make him stop). Some mothers would say "This is a good idea, the children like it. They should have started one years ago" (!) Others wouldn't let their kids come because they were afraid they'd get hurt or dirty or both. On balance though, there was a sense of achievement : it was worthwhile— in spite of press attacks, snobbery and minor crises". "I succeeded in Welwyn because by that time I had found ways of building in controls within the children recognizing them as such". "They felt free".

Jack provided an account of a rough group which he had to expel from the playground, since they disrupted and demoralized the play of the younger children. He followed them home and observed their intense interest in a broken scooter they were not able to fix. Together they opened a scooter club, in which the lads salvaged and fixed discarded scooters, which became the centre-piece of the playground. However, once they got a license and launched the scooters, the activity died out". -Jack Lambert.

There was now a nucleus of regulars and playground helpers amongst the older kids who attended the playground daily at Pin Green. One of the new attractions to the playground was our gerbil which was housed in the new garage near the pet's area; the pet's area now also contained rabbits and guinea pigs. The children's dens ranged from four sided basic play houses with curtains to more elaborate carpet lined mansions of four storey's with trap doors and secret entrances. Children would drift from one group to another, swopping materials or ideas. It was a very cooperative venture and exciting to watch and be part of. The adventure playground became a very democratic sharing community of kids fully absorbed in play. In the evenings the siren sound of the playground capstone would sound loud echoing across the pin green neighbourhood, heralding the playgrounds closing for the day. This was the signal for the return of tools and farewells between children and staff. Soon the playground became still and quiet. We built many new tower extensions including a walkway, a slide, climbing frame, roundabout and a swing made of tires in a pyramid design. All of these were well used, along with the ever popular aerial runway. Although the biggest and most popular activity on the playground was the children's building of their dens. In the main they were constructed from wooden pallets or duckboards, these were rapidly appearing in every corner of the site. It was so encouraging to see so many parents bringing their children to the playground and many of them staying for most of the day. Whilst many also brought their children and called to collect them later in the day. This was an indication of how well the playground was becoming accepted as a safe place, with parents entrusting their children into our care. This was not necessarily an easy option for parents, considering the appearance of the play tower and the tall climbing frames, along with other untidy child orientated activities.

On Saturday mornings and throughout the school holidays there was always a long queue of children waiting to enter at the playgrounds main gate. Once I arrived and undid the padlock and opened the playground hordes of children surged forward and rushed in. Some pushing bikes whilst others were holding hands of young brother or sister and all hurriedly scampering to their chosen area of the site. Whether it was to their den in progress of construction, to the aerial runway, wooden roundabout, slide on the tower or to sit around the barbecue area or wander into the play hut. So that once the majority were inside the grounds the noise was often deafening with constant hammering, sawing or raised Children's voices. Often requesting help from us the play workers or asking a question. Small children snuggling close to us and often enjoying various active games and noisy rhymes. The community involvement was always an essential element, as well as the school holiday play schemes with their added new dimensions. Imaginative leaders added their own ideas, based on what they saw and what they believed best suited the needs of the children. Often these new initiatives grew out of the latest craze, such as bicycle tracks, go carts, bicycle rides, skateboards, or from a similar interest in music such as with a steel bands shed, or a camp fire idea which became the barbecue area. The adventure playground was always growing in ideas, always changing, always meeting the needs of children like the growth of safety racks to lock children's bikes away safely whilst they were on site each day. The need for disco units to cater for the interest in pop music by all ages, the need for a youth section and pre-school area and ultimately the need for disabled access and the social integration of the disabled in the community. Adventure playgrounds themselves had to change their image, although keeping their roots and original ideas; their philosophy remained the same. They became richer in the range of provision; creatively more advanced with the more specialist den building and play structure, bonfires became barbecues and community events, whilst the use of use of waste materials was more selective, though sand and water features were still essential. My own individual way of working with children was to encourage them in their play activities both individually and collectively. To take part in play activities and events of all description, was as I saw it part of the job. A job that encompassed traditional street games and group rhymes, including circle games, action songs, hide, and chase activities, alongside the more organized and very traditional recreational games. Such as rounder's, football and cricket, which were all very essential. Working in this way, I quickly grasped a working knowledge of a wide range of game repertoires, that also included children's chants and rhymes. All gained from all corners of the United Kingdom, both from the inner cities and the country towns. Play workers nationally worked on ensuring and making adventure playgrounds become more and more community oriented during those years. So that they included a variety of new initiatives within them. Even one of its own Bernard McGovern, a play manager in the London Borough of Lewisham and the author of "The Play Leaders Handbook" and "Play Leadership." Distanced himself from many of the radical aims of many play workers employed on adventure playgrounds. By being critical of the view that the play worker should have a high profile role in the community. He felt that a community liaison responsibility detracted from the main task of providing playground activities and led to the perpetuation of a fear that adventure playgrounds were seen by the public as being full of juvenile delinquents. This has not been the case with the vast majority of play people however, or people such as Gyles Brandraith and Virginia Bottomley who became members of Parliament. Whilst Authors like Sue Townsend, of Adrian Mole fame, are now part of this list. *Throughout my years in play work I have been privileged to work alongside or to follow in the footsteps of many outstanding play people. Those who pioneered the world of Child's play. Many of whom I had the privilege to know personally or work with over many decades .* All of these and others in the UK played their own roles in the concept, that of the child's right to play. Whilst it is apparent that earlier reformers and thinkers had influenced them all. Such as the founders of organizations for children's activities, like Lord Baden Powell, with his scout camps on Brownsea Island at Poole in Dorset and A.S Neil of Summer hill originally based at Lyme Regis Dorset. It was Neil whose letter to the London Times had initially sparked off the debate on adventure playgrounds and ultimately which led to their development and growth worldwide. Play work has changed enormously since those initial days, when leaders worked within a very small budget and usually very much alone and with very little managerial support. I and others were able to play the role of a Robin Hood type of enabler, detached and yet involved in providing the perfect environment for the child to test out and try new activities.

Some of the very best play people have not had any formal qualifications, but what they have had has included a natural flair and a special aptitude to be able to relate to children. It is also a fact that many people are not ideally suited to work with children and that others are not ideally suited to working within an unstructured play environment. Such as on an adventure playground, or play leadership scheme. However, the most successful play people have usually been those who possess a healthy enthusiasm for the vocation, endless energy, fondness for children and keenness to work with them in their projects. Along with a positive attitude, a creative mind, along with a confidence in themselves and an interest in and belief in the philosophy of child play. All children need to have adults like play enablers somewhere around if only to read them stories, to sing with them, encourage them and to care for them if they fall and to ensure that their play environment is safe and exciting. Since the very first days of adventure playground there has been great discussions over the role of the person elected to operate these sites. Because of his/her role it was imperative that the name title should represent and reflect the actual role he or she was expected to play.

The numbers attending the playground during school holidays was expected to be high and this year was no exception. During August with between two to three hundred children in attendance daily and their ages ranging from two years upwards. There were many incidents at the playground during my time there. The ones that stand out were notable and include the following.- Brian a regular youth member, tall strong, was involved n one of these free for all gang scuffles. About 8 youths were on the playground floor in a big heap of hands and legs obviously fighting. So when I arrived on the scene they quickly dispersed leaving just one guy on the bottom. He was gathered in a ball and whining "Don't hit me Ray" After reassuring him we went into the office he was tearful, it was then I noticed the bruises on his body and I asked him who he got them .It was then he told me about the abuse with belt beatings from his step father, I of course had no choice but to phone the social services and shortly after a social worker arrived. There was some discussion and then she left with him. Later she came back to inform me it was all lies and he had a lovely home and parents. She seemed more overjoyed with their homes furnishings than anything. That evening he came to the playground and we talked in the office for sometime he told me he had just had another belting and was running away. That evening I was attending the local social services panel of which I was a member and brought the matter to their. They were shocked and assured me they would deal with the matter. Later he received counselling and the trainee social worker was reprimanded. On another occasion the kids came running to me" Quick, quick, Ray, Mick has a big rock and is threatening to beat it on a guy's head". I hurried outside and there was Mick a 14 year old regular, he was a big lad looked a good few yrs older he was holding a giant stone in his arms and threatening a younger boy with it. I had to talk him down from his temper and get him to drop it. Eventually he did, then he burst into tears. I took him in the office and we talked. Mick was to be one of the best workers amongst the youth for I gave him the responsibility for building the play structures he was strong and he became very adept and reliable. On another occasion a young boy was coming to the playground and throwing stones at everyone then running out. This became a problem and I discovered from questioning the kids that he wasn't liked and had B.O. One day I managed to catch him then took him aside for a chat he was obviously thinking he was in serious trouble. After a long chat I persuaded him to look after his personal care and he said he would bath before he returned. When he came next I had persuaded one of the younger girls Tracy to befriend him and over time they became good friends and he became a regular helper with the tots on the playground assisting them with their den building.

A small boy David from the St Nicholas neighbourhood, had walked the two miles to the playground daily. Though he was just aged two, he had just strolled into the site early one evening accompanied by his five year old sister They became involved in the painting sessions in the hut and soon became playground regulars. Pete Lynch the local community policeman who was a member of the playground management committee was a regular visitor. He was well liked and respected by all the youths who would spend hours chatting to him and exchanging banter and jokes. As a result of the success of the "Children Waiting" film and the national Fair Play campaign many new adventure playgrounds started up in all major towns and cities in the U.K. I consider myself to be so fortunate to be involved in play at this buoyant time. Experiments in play nationally were in abundance with a vast variety of schemes nationwide, including full time adventure playgrounds, play centre's, holiday play scheme programmes, play buses, play streets and play sculptures. Projects sprung up in towns like, Telford, Washington, Milton Keynes, Basingstoke New Town and Redditch as well as country areas and inner cities. One pioneer of play leadership, H.S. (Pat) Turner, commented that, "It is a personal job, demanding a personal style, more rewarding than anything else I've ever done". Remarking on the adventure playground concept, Pat said, " It is a living thing, a community with many facets and in constant change". The play leader has to be resourceful to have a quick eye for opportunities to both improve and expand the range of facilities on the site. To be always prepared to provide an abundant range of play materials for energetic and versatile children from timber to scrap materials to game items. He or she must be prepared to intervene as a mediator in situations with and amongst groups and with individual children where there is friction, bullying or conflicts of interests. To step in where there is a likelihood of harm to children causing or receiving physical hurt. A great deal of his time is spent working closely in liaison with other professionals from the play field or the statutory welfare services. Caring professionals from the Social Services, Welfare, Probation, Education, Community Workers, Schools and Youth Workers. This involves the play leader in attending numerous meetings with play people and a wide range of those who work closely with children. The relationship between the leader and each individual child is of great importance, he must know when to help the child, and when to withdraw, so that the child can work at the problem alone and learn confidence through unaided achievement.

At the playground the preschool playgroup children were excited when I arranged regular supplies of sand to be delivered to and dumped at the playground site. They hurriedly ran out and brought their buckets and spades from their homes and it was like a sunny summers day at the beach. I had initially used this concept at the Boscombe play scheme earlier yrs in Bournemouth. The play hut was now used for clay modeling, crayoning sessions, billiards, and snooker and also there was a piano. I displayed a blackboard at the entrance to the site with details of the day's programme, an idea I picked up from working with Pat Smyth at Notting Hill adventure playground in the mid sixties. Jim Jackson was on site each day and took a daily record of numbers attending for the Development Corporation, Jim had like me also had once been a C.S.V volunteer in the sixties. The playground had its own monthly news sheet which I worked to improve, this was run out monthly, printout by the playgrounds secretary, on an old gestetner machine. I changed the newsletter format and called it "The Adventurer" and the children delivered it to local houses. In its first new issue I stressed the importance of the playground children not wearing plim soles on the site, because of the nails from discarded timber etc, from den building activities. This safety inspection was also carried out daily on the playground and a notice no plim soles was displayed at the entrance to the playground. Children who were found wearing plimpsoles were encouraged to go home and change their footwear. Regular trips out organised each week and often on a Saturday there would be long queues of children in the car park waiting for the departure of a double Decker bus, or coach trip to the zoo, cinema, or to London. These excursions were advertised in our newsletter "the Adventurer" and with posters the children had created and displayed in local shops. There were numerous day trips out with up to two double Decker buses packed full of excited kids. On one hot day we visited the Hertford county Show courtesy of the local N.P.F.A offices, although the children spent most of the day fishing for tiddlers, using nets they had bought at the show. The local N.P.F.A county officer and David Kershaw were both very amused by this. As Dave remarked at the time "Provide kids with all the attractions of a county show and they still prefer to play simply in water".

Around the adventure playground barbecue at Stevenage

The playgrounds management committee regularly held a fund raising stall which was run by David Kershaw's wife Enid. This was in the town centre every few weeks situated on the joyride platform in the town square. Socially I was invited to regular wine and cheese parties by Dave and Enid and here I would meet local doctors and other professional people. On one such social occasion I attended a party in the home of Lady Cromer at Cromer Hall. I recall that all of her furniture was antique and the lighting in her rooms were large candles. We continued our constant search for regular supplies of timber and other play materials, which were all necessary for the demands of the children for their many dens and the building by staff and youths of the play structures. Some parents donated and delivered lorry loads of timber daily. Mr and Mrs Woods from the St Nicholas Play Association provided us with a constant source of tree barks courtesy from the forestry commission's mills and Bo-water's supplied the wooden pallets or duckboards. Local donations of equipment for the playground included a variety of stuff including a billiard table from a local dad, an amplifier for the disco unit, two armchairs and table tennis nets. Throughout this month the youths made full use of a partitioned disco area for daily pop music sessions. The disco being created by a local dad Colin Guest with help from some of the older lads, whilst his wife ran the kitchen. There were also coffee sessions each afternoon in the play hut where youths sat and chatted or cooled out. One of the lads with help from some of the others, built a new climbing frame on the site. Some of the younger kids were now involved in the painting of this new attraction, which was well supervised. At the playground a young lady who was training to become a nursery nurse was seconded onto the playground as part of her training and worked with the younger children in the play hut. She had a special flair and aptitude and quickly made a special impact with the toddlers and left the playground with a good reference, to eventually become a qualified local nursery nurse. My playground assistant Andy had built a special wooden parking bay for the children's bikes which had proven a godsend. Andy was now considering leaving to return to his former career in engineering and a local dad Les

132

Lewis ,who had volunteered to help on the site, was considering applying for the position.

At that time the number of adventure playground accidents in the UK was low compared to the conventional hard surfaced play areas, apart from occasional grazed knees from falls. We also made it a point to the kids at the playground that they needed to use padlocks on their bikes for there were many instances of bikes stolen or borrowed and dumped whilst their owners were busy playing on the playground site. A special permanent brick built barbecue with plank seating was constructed in a quiet corner of the site by a local dad, with support from the youths and staff. I had obtained a heavy iron grid as a cooking area. There were many parents who were now regular volunteers they brought their children to the playground daily and stayed all day. A youth member went through a trying time and got involved in car joy riding. He was sent to a detention centre out in the Hertfordshire countryside and his probation officer and I visited him. Later we made arrangements so that one of the playgrounds local family were able to adopt him and keep him on the straight and narrow. The playgrounds fund raising subcommittee led by David Kershaw's wife Enid, provided much need cash for the purchase of barbecue cooking utensils. Through her tireless work on the Joyride in the town centre. The barbecue area soon became the playgrounds main communal social focal point and was always full of chattering happy kids. The regular evening barbecues attracted many new children who brought steaks, bacon, potatoes and eggs. Often I would visit Dr Ron Faulkner his wife Shirley and their children in the Stevenage old town, taking playground regulars Sue and Kevin Riley with me for a day out.

Throughout this time the youths made full use of a partitioned disco area which they had built in the play building for daily pop music sessions. The disco being created by a local dad Colin Guest with help from some of the older lads, whilst his wife ran the kitchen. There were also coffee sessions each afternoon in the play hut where youths sat and chatted or chilled out. One of the lads who had become a regular, Mick McKee, with help from some of the others, built a new climbing frame on the site. Some of the younger kids were now involved in the painting of this new attraction, which was well supervised. Children's dens ranged from four sided basic play houses with curtains to more elaborate carpet lined mansions of four storey's with trap doors and secret entrances. Children would drift from one group to another, swopping materials or ideas. The adventure playground became a very democratic sharing community of kids fully absorbed in play. At one time there was trouble from children entering the playground when closed at night and this was overcome by the council planting special tall and wide bushes with protruding prickles around the perimeter of the playgrounds vertical concrete slat fencing.

As play workers, Les Lewis, David Kerrell and I floated between the childrens many activities in the hut and on the site, ensuring that all was going well. Occasionally breaking up a dispute, sorting out a disagreement or manning the barbecue, or working on the play structures. Such was our role until the late evening, only broken by visits to the kitchen for refreshments, or to the office, to answer a phone call, order timber or attend to first aid. Individual children would leave for tea in the afternoons and return later refreshed. There was now a nucleus of regulars and playground helpers amongst the older kids who attended the playground daily. One of the youths Kevin Rileys dad visited from Australia who was a film director and videoed the adventure playground on film. One of the new attractions to the playground at the time was our gerbil which was housed in the new garage near the pet's area; the pet's area now also contained rabbits and guinea pigs. As a result of the (N.P.F.A) National Playing Fields Associations film "Children Waiting" and the national campaign of Fair Play For Children. During this time many new adventure playgrounds started up in all major towns and cities in the o.k. I consider myself to be so fortunate to be involved in play at this buoyant time. Experiments in play nationally were in abundance with a vast variety of schemes nationwide, including full time adventure playgrounds, play centres, play buses,, play streets, holiday play scheme programmes and play sculptures. Projects sprung up in towns like,Telford,New Town, Washington,Peterborough ,Milton Keynes,Basingstoke and Redditch. As well as in remote country areas and the inner cities of Sheffield, London, Newcastle,Cardiff,Bristol, Southampton etc. There were also at that time an estimated 1,700 holiday play schemes operating throughout the UK during school holidays. Such was the interest and support for Child's play provision nationally mainly due to the work of the (NPFA) National Playing Fields Association and their team of regional play officers. The very first efforts to provide training for play leaders had been sketchy, ranging from crash courses via the (N.P.F.A)The National Playing Fields Association in the mid sixties and day release courses at Kennington College, Stockport Technical College and Goldsmiths. These courses were supported by the N.P.F.A and tutored by Alan Curtis of the N.P.F.A and Virginia Bottomley of the Child Poverty Action Group(Virginia later became a formidable Member of Parliament) Andrew Scott and Tony Chilton. *The two distinct areas of child play, that of play leadership and the adventure play work movement,* came together with the formation of the new Institute of Play Leadership, This body was intended to encompass all of the various play disciplines and Colin Mayne was now tutoring the first full time play course at Thurrock Technical College at Grays in Essex.

With the success of the Stevenage adventure playgrounds, thanks to the earlier work of Donne Buck and others like David Kershaw and Betty Pickersgill. Stevenage was shown as an example how local authority and voluntary community play associations could work together, in encouraging the growth of adventure playgrounds nationally throughout the seventies. At that time the Stevenage Play Association had gained the contract to sell the refreshments at the official day opening of the towns new Fairylands Valley Park, all of the profits to go to the Stevenage Play Associations funds. I was proud to see that so many of our parents from our newly formed pin green parents group were prominent in this venture. On the day they were exceptional, both in numbers and in the work undertaken. All in all this was a great day out for all involved and gave us all a chance to mix socially with members of the various play associations in the town. It was around this time that Andy my assistant left the playground and Les Lewis who was a parent volunteer was officially appointed as play assistant and by now had taken it upon himself for the responsibility of the daily cooking at the barbecue area. The adventure playground had now become a vibrant and exciting community of children of all ages and abilities.

CHAPTER NINE

STEVENAGE AT PLAY

The play hut centre at pin green adventure plaground

We had decided to organize a play carnival for Pin Green with floats and events to raise funds for the (U.N.A) United Nations Association project and for Dr Faulkner's new " Opportunity classes toy library" Which was to be based at Bowes Lyons House community centre in Stevenage town centre. Our carnival procession with 7 its floats paraded throughout the pin green neighbourhood. Whilst the Chief of police gave the orders to close off the roads from traffic and I had to sign a form stating I was totally responsible for the event. Betty Pickersgill from the Canyon Adventure Playground committee and wife of councillor Jack Pickersgill for both Stevenage and Herts worked tirelessly as ever on the project with me. A few weeks later I was invited by Ron and Shirley Faulkner to attend their opening party for their new Toy Library at Bowes Lyons House community centre (which had originally been opened by Lady Bowes Lyon -the

Queen mother). At the party Ron gave a speech and I was officially thanked by him.

The (U.N.A) United Nations Association Handi -camp work party would be involved in creating pathways around the site, for use by handicapped children for access to all the play facilities. It was hoped that the handicapped student's involvement would act as a spur to other handicapped people to use the playground. The committee had approved the idea and I had approached the U.N.A earlier in the year and had met up with Andrew, their U.N.A national organiser. In earlier years I had known Godfrey Leak when he was secretary of the U.N.A and had visited him in his grand offices top floor in the United Nations building on the embankment in London, with its grand spectacular view overlooking the River Thames. The twelve U.N.A HANDI CAMP foreign students would stay in the play building at Pin Green for around a month whilst working on the project. We had found it difficult to find other local accommodation for the students and Les Lewis my play assistant had approached the W.R.V.S and social services and with their help it was resolved. The main difficulty being that the work party should not be split up, as this would defeat the object of the U.N.A project. The students all arrived in late July and stayed until mid August.

The local Webb Rise Special School for handicapped children were already using the playground on a regular basis, along with other children with disabilities and groups, such as Dr Ron Faulkner's " Opportunity Classes ".Often Ron would stroll onto the site with many from his group. We now had fresh new members who joined in signing for a youth section on our petition. These older youths were motorbike enthusiasts or "greasers". Young men who were very willing to take on responsibility for construction work, or as voluntary play assistants. They had become very popular with the preschool children who used the playground, who clung to them and respected and trusted them. I would often go to town with them on the back of their big motorbikes for shopping expeditions. In the evenings they would stay on at the playground to assist me with the clearing up after the youth section closed and help me clear up after a busy day on the playground and then drive me home. It was these lads who were most impressed with the handicapped students courage and determination, despite their physical disabilities. The greaser lads were especially impressed by Mike one of the (UNA) United Nations Association work camp students who was born with just stumps of arms and legs yet threw himself eagerly into the physical work on the site, amazing many of the playgrounds youth members. Some of the UNA students were in wheelchairs and others were able bodied. During this time Pathe News sent a film crew to film the U.N.A scheme for distribution and screening in the Lebanon, care of the Central Office Of Information.

This year 1973 was also the Herts Adventure Play Progress Year known as "HAPPY 73". This campaign was spearheaded by my employer David Kershaw the chairman of the Pin Green play association, Betty Pickersgill secretary of the Canyon adventure playground association and Major Tatham of the (N.P.F.A.) National Playing Fields Association. The campaign of "HAPPY 73 " worked for the growth and development of play in Hertfordshire. Its committee organised a play conference in Stevenage and a Play Day in the town when the town was closed to traffic and the shopping precinct was turned into a play arena for children's activities for a day. A large group of teenagers turned up at the site one day, they were all from the Chells adventure playground who couldn't cope with them. These soon became playground regulars at pin green assisting in the play hut canteen and looking after a few of the tiny tots on the playground. Les Lewis my assistant soon took these youths under his wing helping him with the barbecue campfire preparations and the Guest family who were regulars more or less took them into their family too. The group or gang from Chells very soon became individuals who all took on roles on the playground and became well accepted by the playground regulars.

During the long summer holidays we noticed that a number of the kids were missing out on meals so we members of Stevenage Play Association had discussions with Herts Education department and arrangements were made to provide free school meals on all the adventure playgrounds in Stevenage for children who normally would receive meals during school days. We had a lovely alder tree on the playground which had enormous offerings of berries each year. Jim Jackson would take them regularly on his regular visits and make delicious alder berry wine.

By September the evenings were beginning to draw in and this created a homely atmosphere and special feel about the playground, especially around the bonfires and the regular barbecues. During these days I had been writing a handbook for play leaders which Andy Scott of N.P.F.A asked if they could publish it when completed. Thus this publication entitled "Contacts For Information and Advice in the Community" became one of a series of handbooks published by the NPFA in 1975. Later back at the playground I had a phone call from Drummond Abernethy asking a favour. A newly appointed N.P.F.A Regional officer Andy Scott was coming to Stevenage and Drummomd had phoned me and asked me to make Andy welcome and introduce him to everyone. Andy was a former Adventure playground leader. Following our meet up Andy and I became close friends for many years and he was a regular visitor and encouraged many projects developments in our region over the years. Though when we attended the meetings at N.P.F.A s Playfield House he and Jack Lambert adventure play leader were always up to their tricks with Drummond and often he was not too amused with their pranks.

During the year I made various trips to visit other adventure playgrounds, and attending numerous conferences these are some of these occasions.

A group of us from Stevenage Adventure playgrounds spent a day visiting Bob Hughes adventure playground in Haverhill Suffolk. The Haverhill playground was quite amazing being situated within four high grassy walls. Over the course of some 30 years in play Bob would work with N.P.F.A as well as establishing 3 very different adventure playgrounds as he was to write of later in his book "Evolutionary Play work and Reflective

Analytic Practice". I also travelled to London to attend play leaders meetings at N.P.F.A s Playfield House, or to attend conferences at Central Hall Westminster. Often campaigning with other play leaders from the UK on a variety of issues like " The Lollipop brigade". This Campaign for improved nursery education, was led by Mary Bruce of the Pre School Play Association. National Campaign for Nursery Education organised the Lollipop Lobby. After travelling to London we had marched to Hyde Park for a teddy bears picnic in the park with hundreds of preschool children present. Then afterwards we marched onto Westminster to present a petition to Margaret Thatcher M.P at Downing Street who was then Secretary of State for Education. I led the entourage of mums and toddlers along with play leader Peter Heseltine and I led with the singing of a chant "We want nursery education". Later a petition of 97,000 signatures was handed to Margaret Thatcher by Peter Heseltine of the NPFA National Playing Fields Association asking for Circular 8/60 (which prevented local authorities expanding nursery education provision) to be revoked and Mary Wake was invited in to number 10 by Margaret Thatcher. I visited Rogerstone where I had previously operated the Log Cabin play centre. it was a happy visit as I was settled well in Stevenage at that time. However, it was also a sad day for I was informed that Moira and Clive Ballew had only just returned from a holiday abroad, where one of their two boys had only just tragically lost his life in a swimming accident. On one occasion with Andy Scott I journeyed to Poole to attend a play conference in the south of England at Canford Heath Middle School. There I met up with Sylvia Nash Play Therapist at Poole hospital and Roger Browne Recreation Officer of Bournemouth Council. Roger an old friend who had previously employed me for Bournemouth Borough councils parks department. Where I ran the new holiday play scheme at Walpole road Boscombe Bournemouth a few years previously with support of Roger Browne's wife Jan Browne. When I met up with Roger and Sylvia they told me then that they had plans for me to develop an adventure playground in Bournemouth at sometime in the future.

When I attended the regular and numerous play leaders meetings in London at N.P.F.A Play Field House and (A.P.W.A) Adventure Playground Workers Association at Notting Hill adventure playground during these years. We discussed a great many issues and concerns. However the main concerns which always seemed to crop up were the different philosophies of the play leadership/ play schemes and the adventure playgrounds. It was out of these concerns that adventure play workers had formed their own bodies and organisations such as (LAPA) the London Adventure Playground Association and APWA. As many felt that the Adventure playground leaders were not being taken seriously by being sucked into the more official Play leadership tag. Jim Jackson, Leo Jago, Mike Buckley and Pat Smythe were often prominent at these meetings. The agendas of play leaders held at (NPFA) National Playing Fields Association Playfield house regularly included the need for a proper play structure for play workers who often were employed under numerous scales of social work, youth work or local government. Many play leaders were on very low wages and employed as casuals and not salaried and there were discussions over possible trade union involvement. There were concerns that the adventure playgrounds would be forcibly engulfed into the play leadership philosophy network. As we as adventure playground leaders were more concerned with the community involvement in the Adventure Playgrounds philosophy. I had many discussions with Drummond at this time over these concerns although he felt the strength in unity within play workers and play leaders would make play much more established in the eyes of the government and the public. Hence his drive to establish an "Institute of Play Leadership" and a national diploma course at Thurrock. I was always bringing the issue of the establishment to Drummond at meetings in Westminster central hall. We also were in favour of the social integration of disabled children on playgrounds and the safety of conventional playgrounds with safety surfaces. Other items were discussed at Playfield House many play leaders group meetings. These included the numerous national campaigns, filming of playgrounds and appointments of regional officers of (NPFA) National Playing Fields Association as well as the involvement of press media etc. Groups like "Gold Diggers" and their charitable functions were discussed as well as others sources of income for adventure playgrounds. As well as guidelines for playgrounds staff and the coordination of play associations and the development of regional play associations etc.Many visitors to the offices of (NPFA) National Playing Fields Association at Playfield House and later at 25 Ovington Square over the years included Prince Phillip its President. There were a few early pioneers of adventure playgrounds like Joe Benjamin who voiced their concerns of possible loss to the free play experience of children with the modern adventure playgrounds. Lost to the control; of the play worker/adults with metal swings, slides replaced by wooden play structures of telegraph poles, railway sleepers and metal chains and seating replaced with ropes and tires. "Yet I knew from my own childhood play hood experiences that us kids then had climbed up permanent solid trees and swung from Tarzan swings made from rope and tire or wood seating and that this wasn't the position and provided that adventure playgrounds retained their den building elements I really didn't see any loss in the child's own play experience".

Around this time Drummond Abernethy and Colin Mayne established the Thurrock College Diploma in play work. `Also around that time 1973 I was given the opportunity able to speak at a BBC broad-casted talk at Devonshire House in London. This conference was on the need for the social integration of the handicapped in society at a national conference for, " the social integration of the handicapped ", organized by Kith and Kids. On the platform was Sir Keith Joseph, who was the Minister for Health and Social Security at the time ,he gave a talk on the disability welfare benefits system and the welfare state. I recall that he was given a pretty rough ride at the time by a hall full of young mums who had handicapped children. Later in the year great number of us play leaders attended the national play conference in London, regarding the formation of the new play body "The Institute of Play leadership". A meeting in which hundreds of play people attended from right across the UK. I attended a play conference down south in Dorset at Canford Heath Middle School in Poole and it was there that I first met up

143

with Sylvia Nash Play Therapist at Poole hospital lecture Hall. Sylvia attended the conference with Roger Browne Recreation Officer of Bournemouth Council. Roger was an old friend who had previously employed me at Walpole road Boscombe Bournemouth a few years previously. When I managed the new holiday play scheme there with support of his wife Jan, for Bournemouth borough council parks department. A coach load of us play staff and members of Stevenage Play Association visited Sheffield's Councils for the (IPA) International Play Associations Conference .We spent the day visiting all their adventure playgrounds and attended a candlelit dinner in the evening in the great hall of the council building, courtesy of the Sheffield city council. Here I was to meet up again with old friends Diane Whittaker of the Handicapped adventure playground and Drummond Abernethy once again.

The adventure playgrounds toddlers having fun at the piano in the play hut

"The Fair Play For Children Campaign"

Art picture courtesy of Dawn Jeanette Grant Harrison

A national campaign was led by the Revd Trevor Huddleston, the Bishop of Stepney. Following his letter to the Times newspaper highlighting a boy who had tragically drowned in the Regents canal.

The letter to the Times from the Revd Trevor Huddleston Bishop of Stepney

Sir. "A few days ago a young friend of mine in Stepney, Bobby McNally, aged nine, was drowned in the Regents Canal. Another child of seven was drowned with him. It was the first day of their school holidays. Of course such accidents occur all over the country and in widely differing contexts. Of course, too, the usual pieties and the usual counsels about parental responsibility are mouthed. I wish to state, without apology or qualification, that in this part of London children suffer and die for lack of proper recreational facilities. And I believe this lack, in a country as affluent as Great Britain, to reveal a sinful and scandalous insensitivity on the part of successive governments. Since the Plowden Report it has been recognized that there must be Educational Priority Areas involving more generous financial provision from the state. But, as the recent National Child Development Study From Birth to Seven makes clear . . . " equality of educational opportunity cannot be achieved solely by improving our educational institutions" . It is the total environment that must be changed. The local authority, the local community and many voluntary agencies in East London are doing their best to provide recreational facilities and opportunities during the school holidays. But they are up against vast environmental difficulties in terms of disused canals, dangerous motorways and, above all, lack of open space. I plead on behalf of thousands of children like Bobby McNally for the proclamation of Recreational Priority Areas in the great cities of our land, and for the financial support from Government which alone would make this a reality. Can a country spend £1,000 million on the development of one supersonic airliner for its tycoons yet allow its own children so little opportunity, for the freedom and the safety of proper recreation? I believe that on the answer to this question largely depends the future of our country. I remain, sir, yours truly,

TREVOR HUDDLESTON",
CR, 400 Commercial Road, E1

One of the very first play people to become involved on bomb sites in London was the late Janet Dalglish MBE whose habit of travelling around with a battered suitcase full of junk and other goodies became legendary. Janet was determined to provide training and experience for those who work with children in communities. She was there in the earliest days of the adventure playground movement, Janet ran a wonderful ramshackle centre in Camberwell and was President of Fair Play for Children for many years after the death of Trevor Huddleston who founded it with his letter in The Times of 31st July 1972 (and she was there with him then). Janet worked tirelessly in play for over 40 years.

The (N.P.F.A) National Playing Fields Association arranged filming of the Stevenage adventure playgrounds with funding sponsorship from W.D and H.O Wills the tobacco company. The films summary was by the Revd Trevor Huddleston Bishop of Sepney, although initially Chris Nichol leader of the Canyon adventure playground was involved. As a conseqyence the film showed close ups of Mike Fowler mainly due to the fact that he smoked a pipe. The film was on super 8 film and was called "Children Waiting" it was shown on national TV and used by N.P.F.A and The "Fair Play For Children's" campaign. Despite the national picture, this was a period when even the N.P.F.A. found it difficult to find a group of good London adventure playgrounds, to promote their new film entitled `Children Waiting'. Although Islington Play Association had themselves established 14 successful adventure playgrounds, all fully staffed and operational with up to 8 play leaders to a site. I had been fortunate to have worked on a few of these or to have visited the sites regularly over the years. During this time I attended meetings with Dame Shirley Williams the MP for Stevenage, as a member of the Stevenage Community Council and the St Nicholas Neighbourhood Council. I was most fortunate to have an employer like Dave Kershaw who encouraged me in all of my endeavours. At that time I had a visit from Bob Matthews a former youth from the Balsall heath adventure playground days. Bob stayed for a week at Dave Kershaw's home and helped me at the Pin Green playground during that time. The playgrounds preschool playgroup had now expanded in numbers due to demand for places and as a consequence Mary Wakes assistant Doreen Colum was to open another group in other premises locally in September.

A new garage storehouse was built on the playground site by staff
and parents in September which was used for storage of
preschool play equipment and as a workshop. All of the
playground regulars were involved in its construction, including
the Youths, local dads, John the Hampson park grounds man as
well as David Kershaw and Mr Riley.(Kevin Riley stepdad who
did all the electrical work). We were now making arrangements
for our first organized community bonfire scheduled at the
playground for November the 5th and we hoped to involve all
groups locally, including scouts, guides and children from local
handicapped schools. It was envisaged that local dads would take
responsibility for the fireworks display and mums took
responsibility for sales of refreshments. Whilst the play staff
would supervise the event and the bonfire. We were now
escorting the smaller children home when the playground closed
in the evenings, whilst regular den contests on the playground
proved to be a continuing success each day, with hordes of kids
involved of all ages. There were regular jumble sales which
involved our new local parents group and the youth section and
regular trips to London had been a great feature with visits to

H.M.S Belfast and the Tower of London as well as days out to Knebworth Park and house.

Stevenage adventure playground

CHILDHOOD MEMORIES

Here are a few present day memories of those exciting days from local Stevenage people who were kids on the Pin Green adventure playground then. Courtesy of the Face book page entitled "Stevenage Memories".

Pin Green Adventure Playground in Hampson Park

<u>Pauline Lancaster Market</u>- " At Hampson Park Adventure Playground - I had to give the bouquet of Flowers to Mrs Hampson on the official open day - I think it was 1972".

"I can remember it well I can remember a Ray used to be the boss , and sold the nails."

"We used to make camps from old pallets and pieces of old carpet. We would purchase the nails from the playground office. Health and Safety would never allow it now the boring old sod's, I'm not surprised the kids have nothing to do and spend all their time on x box's. We are all still alive and kicking.... Grrrr"

<u>Phil Green</u> -"Fantastic I was on the Pin Green adventure playground float Alice In Wonderland theme" .

<u>Matthew Williams</u> -"I used to go to Pin green adventure playground all the time in the holidays. Loads of things to do and you were never bored. The only one I remember from there was Adian Jarvis who we would later meet at Sparrows Hearn children's home Nr Bushy".

<u>Jeremy Williams</u> -" I went all the time from 1975 through to 1986 (when I was 16 and too old for it!), the place was full of little camps that people made, some stood for years, including an

impressive 2 story camp with carpets on the floor and walls! I can only remember 2 play leaders, Doreen and Aiden Jarvis (who later became a social worker), I liked sitting in the office with the staff", " Glad we didn't have health and safety back in the 70's...loved this place, all the camps being made by kids, we had hammers and nails, we were trusted with them!"

Sarah Castle"-I think I remember the camp with carpet, was it up a tree? Think I only climbed up there once because I was too scared of heights". "I also remember that there was a playgroup held there in the mornings, I went there mid 70's". " "Yes I remember it. I remember one Guy Fawkes night there was a bonfire and I bullied my brother into taking me with him. We we're allowed to take our own potatoes and cooked them in the embers! I still walk past it when I walk my dog." "Glad we didn't have health and safety back in the 70's...loved this place, all the camps being made by kids, we had hammers and nails, we were trusted with them!"

Jeremy Williams.-"There was one up a tree, but there was also one near to the garages that had an upper floor! Didn't like the place once the BMX track was made! I remember the ping pong table at the far end. And I think the entrance hallway was pitch black, only lit up by purple florescent lights!" "The Adventure Playground is still there with the original building, though the park, Play Centre and Park Keepers hut went a few years ago, but the area roughly looks the same as it did back in the 70's!" " Some of the camps at Pin Green stood for years, and had carpet in them!"

Jeremy Bristow-"I loved that place, proper outdoor recreation, no Xbox etc....no elf 'n' safety, as you said Andrew Paul, hammer, nails an old crate a bit of old carpet, hey presto , a comfy den !"

Colin Stevens- "I used to play in the canyon before it was a designated adventure playground. When I started teaching I took kids to the canyon and the Hampson Park adventure playground. These places were universities of life where kids studied how to be creative, imaginative, independent and to survive. It is such a shame that do - gooders yet again take away children's rights to learn through doing. And we wonder why kids get bored today. Wrap them all in cotton wool seems to be the order of the day. Keep them safe yes, but give them the opportunity to flourish through adventure".

Naomi Williams-"we went there","best days of my holidays and sats".

Sally Fawthrop- "How many health and safety violations can we see their folks?" Pat Clifford - "load's, Sally Fawthrop- !"Didn't kill us though did it ? lol"

Theresa Gillett -"We used to buy bag of nails and build our own camp there wouldn't be aloud now lol" "And your mums old net curtains".

Madeline Marven- "Brilliant, my kids used to muck around in them, we used to have bomb sites when I was a kid, they were brilliant, really dangerous, got the scars to prove it too!"

Mick Simmons-"It's all about statistics & liability it's ruined the adventure of growing up"."When I was a kid we ran around an adventure playground with saws, hammers & nails building camps I'm truly glad I did not grow up in the PlayStation age".Donna McGraw Taylor. -"Ah we had many good times there with you Ray. Sadly the kids of today miss out on so much due to Health and safety etc. me and my sister were reminiscing about this only the other week. Hope you are well and thanks for all the good memories you helped so many people to make".

*The lads eating burnt spuds at the Pin Green adventure
playground campfire*

The Play Leader
The happy sounds of children hard at play,
Welcoming the promise of another new play day,
All waiting at the adventure gates at the break of day,
A figure approaches down the grassy long track,
Miniature bells they do jingle soft upon the breeze,
From flared trouser bottoms and silk cotton sleeves,

Like a long haired troubadour with piper band,
Small children all around him holding hands.
Here he comes at last they shout and cheer,
With the jingled notes of playground keys on ears,
They all run to greet him with no fear,
Amongst all the children gathered here.

He greets them all with smiles and good day,
Followed by others from down the way,
All children so very keen to enter the gates within,
The adventure gates now opening.

At last the key turns in the lock,
Of the iron gates,
In time by clock,
Pushed back and opened wide,
By hordes of children with eager anticipated eyes,

Sweeping past the figure standing there,
And into the adventure playgrounds jungled fayre.
Leading as he does by just being there,
Patrolling playground site for wear and tear,
See the free abandonment of play frenzied activities,
On rope swing tires,
Aerial runways or tower structures great boards of strength,
Whilst the leader stands by just at arm's length.
Assisting advising when asked to dare,
Construction work of playgrounds varied lairs,

Along with games of pretence run and chase,
With kids dressed up in hats and lace,
So many activities in abandonment of time and space,
In childhood's play times of hectic pace.

Then when it's all over and the day is through,
He closes the site for another day,
And walks home through,
Sounds of children contented and waving all their goodbyes,
With his hands held tight,
By two small fry, Escorting him on his merry way,

The chattering of play of another play day.

Ray Wills

Many parents were now visiting the Adventure playground regularly and chatting with the staff. With close on twenty children's dens on the site, all at various stages of development, this was a sure sign of success. In October Ist I had written in the newsletter, " That when local people talk of the adventure playground and the preschool play group they often see them as separate departments", " Were as, in fact they are not"." The preschool play group is in fact the vitally important part of the adventure playground, its future"." Play being an educational and socialising process. That continues throughout the child's life." As the days became shorter with less hours of sunlight and the cold weather and bleak days of winter arrived the numbers of children attending the playground fell dramatically. The colder days and dark nights made it more difficult for small children to attend, although at weekends numbers were still high. This was particularly so on sunny days. However in contrast, the numbers of teenagers attending the site had greatly increased, with many coming from the Chells neighbourhood. Elaine from the youth section now took responsibility for the pets area, their cleaning, feeding and general upkeep. Whilst Georgina and Peta Seymour, took charge of refreshment sales in the play hut kitchen and Mick McKee for the play construction and safety on the playground. Richard, Chris and Jeff took it upon themselves daily for handing out the tools and for nails distribution. They took on this role and duty seriously by building their own especially constructed tool shop on the site fr this purpose and collecting them in later. November arrived and the community bonfire and fireworks display held on the playground on November 5th attracted in excess of 500 people. All the local community were involved including both Hill top and Webb Rise schools.

Many representatives of national play bodies were paying regular visits to the Pin Green adventure playground at this busy time. These groups included "Fair Play for Children," "Herts Handicapped Association" and the (.P.F.A.) National Playing

Fields Association. Regular play Leaders meetings were held at all the various playgrounds, Pin Green, Bandley Hill, Chells and the Canyon. Whilst recreational games between all of the schemes took place on all the adventure playgrounds. Andy Scott the regional officer of the N.P.F.A had now become a regular playground visitor throughout these times, supporting all of the playground activities and we became good friends. Coach loads of people journeyed to the playground from various parts of the UK during this time. These included members of various play associations, development corporations, community groups, colleges, universities, local government bodies and play leadership organisations. Along with other interested individuals from various parts of the UK. One visitor, a lady from Morden Peckham London, showed me her photo album of pictures from pre war years. Of kids dressed in long dresses and laced up boots, building play dens in her back garden at Morden in Surrey Joe Benjamin also was aware of this first UK adventure playground. As he wrote of this playground in one of his books on adventure playgrounds "Grounds For Play".

Then one sunny summers day I was invited to give a talk at the nearby Sishes (Y.W.C.A) Young Woman's Christian Association centre in St Nicholas, to a large coach load party of visitors from a university. Then following a successful talk I then invited them over to visit the pin green adventure playground. When they arrived they stayed for quite a while, they were totally amazed at the activities and the community feeling and took lots of photos of kids at play. Around this time a group of parents from Aylesbury visited us including Jill a reporter from the Aylesbury Gazette. Jill would visit us weekly with a coach load of parents and children often spending a whole day with us bringing packed lunches, or joined in our barbecue meals. The Aylesbury Gazette published a special edition which included a full six page spread on the subject of play for H.A.P.P.Y 73 with photos of Stevenage adventure playgrounds throughout. Reporters and photographers from Stevenage Gazzette also came on a regular basis. This was especially so during school holidays to take photos and write articles. The adventure playground concept of catering for a mixed age group provided opportunities for older children to support the younger in many ways with projects and with the organization of trips out from the site. The tiny tot was often being led or supported by a teenage girl, or a large lad on an aerial runway, or else going down a slide together. These were regular daily features of such exciting play environments. The daily planning and organization of the adventure playgrounds activities were all part of the job, in a day in the life of the adventure playground leader. Until recent times, all adventure playgrounds included pursuits such as den building and campfires, as an essential part of their successful framework. Whilst both forms of play with leadership and adventure play, can often be operated running parallel, side by side. With the children attending both styles of activities, such as adventure playgrounds and with play schemes operating close by, or on site. In such situations children have a wider choice and variety of activities available to them. They can choose the activity that suits their needs on any one particular day. Having been successful in establishing and operating both styles of play work venues over the years I am able to see the benefits to children of both. As well as being able to present a view of play with leadership which encompasses the best of both worlds.

The lady planning officer from Milton Keynes Development Corporation visited us and consulted with me, taking my advice on play design for their new town Adventure playgrounds. A large group of play leaders from Islington London also visited us regularly from St John's Wood adventure playgrounds. They were amazed that we could cope with such large numbers of children and yet with only a few members of staff, whilst they had 8 or more full time play leaders at that time and 15 at their peak. Miss Mary Tabor from the Herts Handicapped Association was now a frequent visitor and supporter of the playground. Mary was originally the towns first Housing Officer many years earlier. Parties of scouts, cubs, Guides and brownies attended regularly joining in with our barbecue and social functions. The work on the site by the "U.N.A HANDI CAMP" work party proved to be a great success. I had at one time visited Godfrey Leak in London at his UNA offices overlooking the Thames. Much of its concept had been due to the work of the Stevenage

Play Council by their support of the play carnival in pin green. Visitors to the playground also included Mr Kermode the local Education Welfare Officer who was extremely supportive. Other regular visitors and supporters included Pru Leach, a local social worker, Michael Halsey a lecturer in Social Studies from Hatfield Polytechnic and Dr Ron Faulkner who brought his own children who joined in the activities. The Youth Section for the adventure playground was now officially approved by the Herts county council and a part time worker Peter Johnson was appointed. It was to be open for two evenings a week initially, Sundays and Tuesdays. It would have its own management committee consisting of youth section members and Les Atkins would be its chairman. It was known as Hampson Youth Club and its age range was from fourteen to eighteen.

I had enjoyed my time at Pin Green Adventure Playground and seen it develop from a small project to a very big community scheme. I had decided now was the best time to leave the playground in the hands of capable staff, Les Lewis and David Kerrell to develop further. I had always been a pro active play worker. Out there involved in structure building or attending to any concerns which might crop up time to time. I was always inclined to go out with the kids on the their outings and to supervise any particular organised activity on site or in the community. Were as Andy liked to stay on the site and was not be one to go out on trips or to organise and Les also preferred to run everything from the office and be on the phone to suppliers apart from supervising the barbecues on the site. Adventure playgrounds needed to be continually growing with new ideas and new leadership. Now I felt it was time for me to move on to face new challenges elsewhere. Of course I was to miss the Pin Green adventure playground, its vibrant healthy kids, challenging youths and supportive parents. A playground where I had actually experienced that which Abraham Maslow the social psychologist described as "The peak experience". Adventure playgrounds such as at Pin Green were rare jewels, they grow out of good seeds planted in the minds of children and adults. They are nurtured and thrive on commitment, adventure and the flair of good play staff and the commitment of local communities. And so it was that adventure play happened at Pin Green adventure playground and it made its mark on many. Other fresh play challenges after leaving Pin Green awaited me but Pin Green adventure playground was really the most exciting place to be in those extraordinary times.

CHAPTER TEN

CHILD'S PLAY IN SKELMERSDALE AND REDDITCH

Art picture courtesy of Dawn Jeanette Grant Harrison

The Drifter and the Gypsy

He was a drifter and a gypsy
strolled into Delphi's own land
he loved the woodlands songbirds
the children held his hands

His roaming days were numbered
yet his smile was strong and true
he lived amongst the gentle folk

and he came from Dorset's Poole

He gathered all the gangs then
who gathered on the town
there were youths with bell bottomed trousers
and children who just had run from mum

The scousers told their stories
to the drifter every day
on the playground in the valley
where the rabbits freely played

The concourse sold its wares there
amongst the new town throng
there were memories of Keegans days
with pigeons hooting songs

The darts they flew in numbers
the catapults were rich
there were many children laughing
amongst the playgrounds ditch

The memories were handsome
with farms so long gone
were tractors rolled the meadows lands
and the dialects was strong

The markets still met up there
where the scousers moved in free
from dingles favorite roaming lands
to skelmersdales own leas

The gypsy drifter walked the lanes
where the blackbirds sang each day
within the playgrounds sanctuary
where the kids so love to play.

Ray Wills

Shortly after I left Stevenage I returned to London for a while
setting up a new adventure playground at Hammersmith and
advising on play centre's for Kensington and Chelsea Play
Association. Where I also sat on the Notting hill playground
Notting hill carnival carnival committee. Shortly after I returned
to Dorset to work for another term at the Carey schools camp at
Wareham. Whilst applying for a new advertised post as
adventure play leader for the social development team and
Barnardos at Skelmersdale in Lancashire. Where I was to be
appointed along with former teacher and youth worker Julian
Finch.

The Delphs Adventure Playground.

The project was a dual scheme between the Skelmersdale
Development Corporation and Dr Barnardos North West Region
office upper parliament street in Liverpool. The growth of the
new towns in the U.K provided a much needed and fresh impetus
to the play movement. Opportunities to develop imaginative
schemes and the development corporations worked closely with
councils. At an earlier time in its history the proposed site was a
natural play area for children's play in the heart of the rural
countryside. It was here that children had played hide and seek,
bird nesting, built dens etc. However in recent times it was used
for more illicit pastimes such as glue sniffing, drugs and
truanting. The Delphs was also famous for the scene of a tragic
accident. A child was drowned playing there in the old quarry. As
a result the quarry was filled in and the site was earmarked for
future development of a child's adventure playground. Julian
Finch was also interviewed and eventually we were both
employed to operate the adventure playground in a dual role. At

the interview one of the panel members presented a miniature model of a playground structure joined with string and asked my opinion. Tony Chilton Regional Officer of the (NPFA) National Playing Fields Association was present and he was quite amused when I answered "It won't last very long on the playground." Julian and I both shared an office within the new social development department building. I would also attend the social development team meetings there and sit on the Barnardos north west team meetings of social workers in Upper Parliament street Liverpool each month. This employment arrangement was quite unique. Attending meetings, writing reports and memos were essential requirements of the work. Once we were appointed and commenced work we both chose to work in detached roles on the estate and in the Delphs woodlands area. Getting to know the kids and youths of the area and build up community contacts. For many months we involved the youths of the neighbourhood in a number of projects to build up their trust. The most successful being the very first community bonfire and fireworks event to be held in the area.

Julian Finch worked closely with the local schools and involved the R.O.S.L.A pupils from the St Richards Comprehensive school These were pupils who now had to stay on that extra year until they were 16 years of age. These pupils stayed with us on the playground site in the Delphs for the whole of the school days during term time. I had to sign an education department form each day for them to attend. One of the projects they were involved in was the dismantling of the farm building from an estate site geared for housing development. These huge barns had formerly been in use as chicken houses or pig sties. We arranged for the transportation of these buildings from the farm to the Assistant Social Development Officers country farm for temporary storage, as play material for the adventure playground structures at the Delphs later. Both the ROSLA school pupils and the kids from the streets of Skelmersdale were involved in this enterprise. All of these kids were involved with the bonfire and fireworks events and activities. We paid visits to the office of the local council West Lancs Play Officer gaining his support and he kindly provided us with a gift of a large supply of fireworks for the display at the bonfire event. Many young people and local parents assisted with building the bonfire and also building a barbecue on site for the refreshments. Others quickly were taking responsibility on the night for refreshments sales and supervision. Many contacts were being built between us and groups such as Birch Green play schemes, local youth clubs and the Ecumenical church centre. Julian and I spent many hours working in the Birch Green and the Tan House neighbourhoods developing new community initiatives such as play schemes, youth clubs and disco clubs. In these ways we were able to build sound relationships with young people and community leaders, local community associations, residents groups and schools and involved them all in our projects. The (NPFA) National Playing Fields Association were actively supportive of the adventure playground with Tony Chilton the N.P.F.A Regional Officer involved as a member on the steering body from its conception. Tony was previously the leader of the highly successful Blacon/Chester Adventure Playground at Chester and in later years he was to become N.P.F.A Play Officer for Wales (the Blacon adventure playground is still functioning today). Julian and I found ourselves attending numerous meetings in the various meeting rooms scattered around the town for opportunities to meet up with new resident and community groups were an essential part of the job. Within the support of members of the social development team such as Keith Cranwell we quickly built up a good contacts. Keith's role was to be actively involved in forming and assisting new community groups in the town. When I first came to live in Skelmersdale I spent a few weeks at a farm house. This was situated on the outskirts of the town. It was the home of the assistant social development officer who was away on leave. I lived here with Keith Cranwell at the time he was in later years eventually to become the Tutor of the play work Diploma course at Goldsmiths University in south London.

Whilst living in the farm house we took responsibility for the care of the Billy goat, who would often get himself tangled up in the brambles and his metal chain. In our spare time I would join Keith for soccer in one of the indoor sports centres, or visit the new crèche in the shopping precinct. Whilst employed in the social development team I undertook a Study into Child's play in the new town, the local playtime pastimes of the Skelmersdale children. This was based on our work with the kids informally on the streets and was entitled "Play in Skelmersdale". The town was badly designed in many ways with lots of concrete slabs and although there was grassed areas these were often not used due to the problem with the clay especially after rainfall. The Skelmersdale children had numerous hobbies some were traditional such as being pigeon fanciers associated with their original rural village life. During the bird nesting session in the spring local kids still went bird nesting which was still illegal and used. Others loved to go tracking in the Delph woodlands or were members of the scouts or guides. Other children made hastily built impromptu go karts often from discarded shopping trolleys, or bread trays from the concourse supermarket. Many youngsters played soccer often under the florescent lights of the subways way into the nights. Whilst many others roller skated around and about the subways and concrete footpaths of the new town. Mountain bikes were also very popular during this time and most kids rode one. The West Lancs councils local groups and the Skelmersdale development corporation ran a variety of schemes which operated throughout the school holidays which were well used. These included discos, youth clubs, leisure centre and a variety of play schemes projects held in the various meeting rooms of the new town. Ian one of our volunteers often took on lots of responsibility at the various clubs Julian and I ran. He was very popular and became the local treasurer of one of the groups in the meeting room. Often the youth members would drop in at my home to share their fish and chips. Even on my birthday they all arrived totally unexpected along with Bill one of the volunteer leaders from the Birch Green community group. We had a great evening with guitar playing and singing till late at night. I recall the rendition of "in my Liverpool home" which was very popular at the time. For the majority of families in Skelmersdale had their roots in Liverpool.

In later years 1988 Tony Chilton wrote that "The primary function of an adventure playground is to help to create an atmosphere which is child cantered; where there are no meaningless limitations or restrictions, apart from precautions necessary against injury; where guidance and help is given when asked for or needed. The relationship between the play worker and individual children is of great importance: they must know when to help a child and when to withdraw so that the child can work through a problem with or without assistance and this develop confidence through co-operation and self-help."

Julian and I attended the Stockport Technical College (N.P.F.A) National Playing Fields Associations play leadership course each week which Tony Chilton tutored. Tony was someone I have always admired a great deal for his articulate wit and skills in Child's play. The play leadership course syllabus included, child development, social studies, psychology, welfare rights and play philosophy. The Stockport course gained much from the experienced play leaders involved and the work of N.P.F.A. Whilst attending the course we regularly visited Tony's former adventure playground at Blacon in Chester for the area play association meetings. Having worked with him to establish the North West Region Play Association. I was extremely impressed with the Blacon adventure playgrounds atmosphere and its team of play leaders. In many ways it reminded me of my previous adventure playground at Pin Green in Stevenage. Whilst on the course with Tony we also attended a Training Day at Blackpool for a drama workshop which was great fun. We visited all the adventure playgrounds in the region at Stoke, Chester, Hulme in Manchester and at Moss side. Moss side also ran very successful holiday play schemes where my friend Margaret Sunderani from Bournemouth was leader for many years. Whilst attending the (N.P.F.A) National Playing Fields Associations Stockport course Tony requested the students to call out their qualifications and he soon had the chalk board full of their many qualifications. He called in the college Principle who after seeing the list on the board told us ours was the most academic standards of students attending the college at that time. Around this time there was great concern over the issue of the tragic death of the child Maria Colwell and I was how chosen by the students on the course to write to Frank Allaun the local Manchester member of parliament on our behalf with signatures and newspaper cuttings. Suggesting that there should be a children's Ombudsman to overlook such cases on behalf of all children. Later Frank took up the issue in parliament through his private members bill, which was approved and implemented in parliament later in 1976.

In Manchester by the late '70s the local authority had decided to close all of the Adventure Playgrounds in the City the week before the long school summer holidays were due to begin due of its view of safety of such sites. Fortunately at the last hour the Council was "persuaded" at a specially convened meeting, to reverse its decision through a sensible and obvious argument suggesting that children were more likely to come to harm if left to wander the streets in search of adventurous experiences, rather than by being on the staffed sites.

The planning of the adventure playground site itself was another area where the leader with the children's involvement could design the layout of the play hut. With its rooms, facilities and the various areas on the site for specific styles of activities. Facilities such as, pre-school play areas and den building areas, the hard surface ball game area, barbecue area, and of course the entrances and exits and services to the site itself. The imaginative and creative play leaders designed such abstract and imaginative sites to meet the needs and energies of creative and energetic children of all ages and tastes.

In 1975 Julian Finch and I invited many community groups in Skelmersdale to take part in a Wild West Show in the Delphs on the playground site as part of the playground open day activities. This included cracking guns, lassos demonstrations and bangers, all very realistic. We laid on a barbecue and refreshments on the day which was a great success. Thanks to the support of the West Lancs District Councils play officer. Meanwhile progress was made with the new play building. Once on the site and over a matter of weeks the building was linked to services, fitted with electrical lighting and then decorated by local parents and children. Solid playground towers and structures were created on the playground using the timber we had stored on the farm as well as telegraph poles. All with practical help of local council workmen and playground youths. The adventure playground was now taking shape, many children were creating a variety of dens in trees within the site. Around this time after over a year at Skelmersdale I was also aware of new play developments elsewhere. At Balsall Heath in Birmingham the St Pauls Venture Project had taken over the responsibility for my former playground the Malvern street adventure playground. Which was now extended to include a city farm. During these years my friend and former employer Bill Pilcher the Parks Superintendent at Redditch had always kept in close touch and had previously informed me that Redditch would soon be advertising for its first adventure playground leader. The post was to establish a new adventure playground in the new town and to oversee a town wide holiday play Programmes. This was to be an opportunity I was to find hard to resist. Having had my play roots in Redditch years earlier and my dream was to one day establish an adventure playground there. During my formative years in play work Redditch Council had sponsored me to attend a (N.P.F.A) National Playing Fields Association play leadership course in London. Redditch held a place in my heart where the families had made me welcome and invited me into their homes for teas. Particularly the Cook family. With suppers of fish and chips or on fruit picking expeditions to Bromsgrove I discussed this opportunity with Julian and after lots of feedback I made the decision to apply for the new Redditch post. For the Skelmersdale adventure playground was now a reality and I felt Julian had the capability to make it a great success. Plus he had a strong parent body and loyal volunteers along with many playground regulars. I attended the interview some months later at Redditch and was appointed by Redditch Borough Council. Just prior to leaving the Skelmersdale post. I was asked to attend a special meeting in the Social Development Departments offices. At the meeting I was rather surprised that even the cleaning lady was in attendance. I was totally unaware of the reason for such a meeting. Mr Norman Pritchard the Social Development Officer addressed the meeting and gave a speech thanking me for all my work and wishing me future success at

Redditch and in my future. Then I was presented with a farewell present on behalf of the team.

Redditch Play Programme

At Redditch I was responsible for the town wide play programme. These consisted of ten play schemes manned by 120 play staff to operate in 6 meeting rooms, 4 schools and 1 private house in Dudley and 1 play barn throughout the school holidays. The Dudley play scheme had been operating successfully for a number of years. It was led by a local Dudley lady and was based in her home which opened out onto the recreation ground. In many ways it was independent of the rest of the schemes. One of its youth play staff went on in later years to attend the Diploma course in play work at Thurrock Technical College. One of its children in attendance at the play scheme in those days was Lenny Henry who in future years went on become famous as a TV personality and comedian. Amongst the play staff appointed who were in the main teachers I persuaded the council parks superintendent Bill Pilcher to employ a few local mums including Mrs Cooke who had worked with me in previous years when I ran the original play schemes there in the mid sixties. Nick Balmforth of the N.P.F.A Midlands Regional Play officer thought that I was perhaps taking too much on as coordinating all of the play schemes and establishing an adventure playground in the town. However I saw it as a challenge.

The town wide schemes catered for the out of school play needs of children in the age range of six to fourteen years of age. Facilities and resources also utilized included the towns sport and leisure centre, towns theatre and the Disco centre. The play activities would range from recreational pursuits to art and craft pastimes. Each scheme to encourage community participation. Activities included sports, drama, fun days, disco parties and day excursions. Providing enjoyment for children along with a welcome break for parents during the long school holidays. I was involved in interviewing the play staff and persuaded the council to employ local mums as well as teachers to create a balanced team. I worked on providing a package of material for each play scheme containing contacts, resources and networking ideas as well as details of organizing activities. Unfortunately the councils original plans to develop a new adventure playground never materialized, due to council budget cuts. I had an office in the councils sports and leisure centre and had to co ordinate all the schemes within a full play and leisure programmed. I made visits to all the venues to meet the caretakers to ensure there were sound relationships. Regular discos sessions were held at the "Cloud Nine" Disco centre which all the schemes used daily and where I also assisted with the disco unit, which was good fun. Plus there were sessions at the Redditch swimming bath and a variety of sports and leisure activities held each day at the sports and leisure centre along with drama workshops at the towns theatre courtesy of equity and at many of the play sites. The numerous inter scheme competitions were very successful culminating in the final day event at the end of the play programme when all of the schemes children were involved in a sports day knockout competition at the Sports and Leisure Centre. This had taken a lot of planning for many coaches were used throughout the weeks ferrying children around the various activities around the town. It had been hard work but I had enjoyed the challenge. The play programme had involved thousands of children and much of my time had been spent visiting all the various schemes. Meeting play staff, school caretakers and parents as well as liaison with all the agencies involved. All in all the scheme was a great success with so many activities and children of all ages involved daily. After the holidays and the schemes came to an end I was offered the opportunity to stay at Redditch and work within the Parks department, but I felt that measuring children's static play areas was not for me. In November I organised a community bonfire at the Match borough Estate in the neighbourhood where I lived. Shortly after, I left Redditch, to return to Dorset.

During these years I made regular return visits to the Balsall Heath adventure playground and I once again met up with Rob Wheway and with many of the families of the area once again. I also visited some of the youths who had surprisingly kept the farewell letter I wrote to them when I left the playground. Tom was now a local electrician and D.J and Eugene Donnelly worked as a train driver for British rail. Balsall Heath play site was now part of a much bigger community project known collectively as The St Paul's Venture Project .When I visited the Venture the play staff couldn't believe that I was Ray Wills. For although I am 6 two tall, the kids had told them stories and that I was in fact a giant and well over 7 feet tall. Then whilst visiting the Warrens family there was a timid knock on their door Margaret Warren answered it then came to tell me a small boy was asking to see me. I went to see him and let him in, he couldn't have been no more than 5 years old he said "are you Ray Wills?" I said yes and he put his hand out for a handshake and said "I'm very pleased to meet you".

At that time in London's Tower Hamlets the Weavers Adventure Playground was started up by a group of parents on bombed weavers' cottages and officially opened. The play worker Tracy Salmon played here as a child. Like many of the best playgrounds, the structures were and still are kids-built and constantly changing. Timber is scavenged and donated and they still collect junk for building. At one time it was famous for its TV themed structures and sculptures and Brian Cant from the children's TV programme Play away made a VIP guest visit and Until 1990 the playground was also a city farm. However the Thatcher years had brought with it the denial of the concept of society and the abolition of the Greater London Council, which resulted in a massive cull of these valuable and well loved spaces. Structures and Play workers were made to conform to arbitrary, externally manipulating agendas which were not informed by Play work practices or theories. The Adventure Play movement found itself in a reactionary position and floundering for words, a confirmation to those in positions of authority, who were seeking it, that this was a nonsense and a luxury and funding was withdrawn across the board.

At that time I had attended an unsuccessful interview for a position with Glasgow Play Association where I was interviewed by a group of Nuns who made up the committee of the Glasgow Play Association. For me this was quite an unusual experience.

CHAPTER ELEVEN

THE FERNHEATH ADVENTURE PLAYGROUND

Paddy Williamson Secretary and Ted Taylor Youth and Community leader with supporters of Fernheath adventure playground

In the autumn of 1975, I was busy with Robert Whitty managing the Y.M.C.A Crusader youth centre at Bovington Camp near Wareham Dorset.Here we were operating a full programme of activities for local young people. It was then that I was first contacted by Mrs Paddy Williamson Secretary of the Fernheath Play Association and invited for interview for the post of adventure playground leader for Fernheath play association. I met up with her and the play association members and shortly after started work in the west Howe area. My friend Rob Whitty who had assisted me at the Bovington (Y.M.C.A) Young Men's

Christian Association was also appointed as assistant play worker at fernheath adventure playground. Throughout the winter months Rob and I met up with other community leaders, built up contacts and resources and continued to meet local kids informally on the estate. In the spring the association advertised for and interviewed prospective additional staff for the play scheme and playground during the Easter holidays. Two were appointed being Jeff Meddle and Dave Robinson. The Easter holiday play scheme was a great success attracting a large number of children. With lots of functions, trips out and activities throughout with longer opening times due to extra staff cover. Local parents joined in lots of activities and trips to Hengistbury head, Maiden castle and camping at Carey schools education camp in Wareham. We held sports activities on the co op playing fields at West Howe with marked out cricket pitches, football, rounder's and also games of netball within the hard surface games area. There were also many team games and kids games like oranges and lemons, stuck in the mud and action games which I had learnt at Carey school camp. The proposed adventure playground area was also used for ad hoc games and barbeques. Though no actual den building took place as yet. We were still in the process of building a network resources for materials such as wooden palette duckboards etc from nearby Wallisdown industrial estate. One of the first playground projects was to be the construction of the playground fence which was to be a wooden bark paneled fence. This came via the Forestry Commission in the New Forest. The actual work was undertaken by the local Oakmead school sixth form pupils supervised by Ted Taylor the detached youth worker. I knew Ted Taylor from my work in Walpole road play scheme at Boscombe a few years earlier whilst Ted was leader at the nearby school youth club. In more recent years Ted was to become councillor and Mayor of Bournemouth. Once the fence was built we began to utilize the enclosed area, spending more of our time on the site.

We chose June 19th for the official opening of the adventure playground to link in with the national play day of "The Fair Play For Children Campaign 76" date. I contacted the London offices of the (N.P.F.A) The National Playing Fields Association and

Fair Play For Children on a regular basis then, obtaining a mass of publicity material for the national campaign from Sue Kearsley. I also took on the voluntary role of Southern Regional Officer for the National Play Day, passing on information to local and area play associations, such as Poole Play Council and Walpole road play association and Southampton Play Association. I approached the local press and media as well as making contact with an old friend and colleague Jack Lambert the Author of the book "Adventure Playgrounds". Jack was never totally happy with the book felt it had been over edited. He was now Play Organiser at Basingstoke and he was pleased to be invited to our event and to be involved in our official opening coming along to the event on the day with his own decorated Play Bus. During his time there were literally thousands of play schemes operating throughout the UK. It was mainly due to the (NPFA)s National Playing Fields Association system of having such great Regional Play Officers throughout all 7 areas of the UK . Providing area team support and training courses along with supporting new initiatives.

I arranged a day visit to Stevenage with members of the Fernheath play committee and staff visiting all of the towns playgrounds. A visit I had arranged with my friend and former employer Dave Kershaw who was by then Play Officer for Stevenage Borough Council. Pin Green Adventure Playground in Stevenage had by then appointed new play staff and had a new solid play tower constucted on the site.

Back in Bournemouth work on the Fernheath adventure playground began on building dens involving staff, children and parents, with the parents who were often on site all day with their children. On such a warm summers evening Nigel Jones was to involve himself in construction work with his children Wanda and Jai and was to become an active committee member and of the play team. The parents from the play association were now still actively operating the local play associations charity shop at Wallisdown and this along with their other fund raising schemes helped to cover a lot of the play expenses. The Bournemouth council parks department provided a one off grant for holiday staff and the (N.P.F.A)National Playing Fields Association who also provided a one off setting up grant. Paddy Williamson the playground secretary made contact with the local MP Sir John Eden and he had become our playgrounds patron. I sent him regular playground newsletters along with progress reports. We put together our own newsletter "The Adventurer" which the children delivered by hand to local residents, Sir John agreed to open our adventure playground on June 19th as patron of the adventure playground. Following meetings with social services at the local Hyde road area offices. The Fernheath scheme attracted regular visits by social workers and councillors like Mrs. Clifton and George Spicer. The play association held regular monthly meetings at the Henry Brown centre as well as frequent meetings of staff at Paddy Williamson's home and occasionally at the flat the play staff had moved into locally at Talbot Woods. The local probation officer Alan Marsh attended our meetings and was a great supporter and a trainee probation officer Graham Meadows was seconded to the scheme. Later during the busy summer period a local Dad Nigel Jones was to join us as a full time volunteer. Whilst another local man was seconded to us under a community service order. On a visit to Woolworth's in Bournemouth town square, Rob and I persuaded their manager to donate a large pretty boxed doll to the play day raffle. The scrounging of materials for playgrounds from companies and industrial units etc has always been an important aspect of the job. A visit to W.H Smiths in Bournemouth resulted in us using a section of their shop for a display of children's poems and pictures on Child's play. Whilst Zebra Caterers at Wallisdown donated a large bottle of champagne for our playground raffle. The local pub on the estate "The Smugglers Arms" kindly donated boxes of crisps for the day and the local Kinson bakery where one the mums worked provided cakes. So much good will was out there in the community it was so obvious that people and organisations liked to contribute.

When the day of the official opening of the adventure playground finally arrived it was a sunny morning. The activities on the site began with a make-up and fancy dress session competition. Then with the arrival of my friend and colleague Jack Lamberts (author of Adventure Playgrounds)from Basingstoke with his Play bus, fully decorated with banners and balloons. Then there was a carnival parade around the streets of West Howe estate, this consisted of five floats, play bus and children and adults in fancy dress. I was dressed in a jesters outfit, over 80 children took an active part in this event. Later in the afternoon the adventure playground was officially opened by the president of the fernheath play association Sir John Eden MP. John gave an impressive speech as follows ."The adventure playground idea is a creative, constructive experience for children" . He continued to develop this theme with particular reference to the Adults conception of child's play such as toys and the child's use of wood and nails. He made reference to the unnecessary deaths on the roads and accidents in our homes. Then he cut the ribbon at the entrance to the playground and the children entered their adventure playground site, as hundreds of balloons were set free for children to chase. It was indeed a noisy occasion' John then walked across and shook my hand warmly and told me just how much he had enjoyed reading my playground newsletters. The children were led to tables and chairs the parents had assembled where they sat down and tucked into ice cream and fruit. Later that day a pets show was judged by local councillors Mrs. Clifton and George Spicer. The children bringing a large number and variety of pets from their respective homes. Including, cats, dogs, birds and reptiles. Later there were pony rides courtesy of staff from Longham stables, along with sports activities like crazy sports, a barbecue, trampoline rides, storytelling session, a preschool playgroup, kids lucky dips, raffles, refreshments and activities in the sports pavilion. Despite the poorer weather in the afternoon the event attracted a few hundred people and was a great success. Numerous local organisations had been involved in the day's events and programme. Around that time I visited Jack Lambert Basingstokes Play Officer and his wife and children in his New Forest cottage situated in the woodlands in Little Dumner near Basingstoke. Jack was then retiring from many years in Play and concentrating on setting up his own table making business.

The adventure playground at Fernheath was now opening from 3.30pm to dusk daily and on Saturdays from morning to dusk, whilst Sundays we operated from morning to 5.30pm. During school holiday periods we were able to open from 9.30am to 5.30pm daily. My days spent working on the playground were very similar in many aspects to those I had on other adventure playgrounds I had been involved with. There were a variety of chores, functions to arrange. From scrounging play materials, planning programmes, organizing meetings, phoning contacts and resources, organizing days out, checking play equipment for safety as well as ordering new play equipment. to be resident DJ for the evening and a great many local youths attended this noisy event. We paid a visit to the Poole Marine Centre at Hamworthy Poole where we managed to obtain a regular supply of rope and commando nets for the playground. This summer of 1976 was exceptionally hot, most of us play staff were now well tanned, for the adventure playground site seemed to trap the heat. On the hottest day Rob and I had planned a fundraising walk to raise monies for the scheme, when we walked to Bovington and back some 28 miles. One sunny day Ted Taylor and a group from South Kinson Sports spent the day putting up a new climbing frame on the site. Throughout this sunny summer the noise of children's hammers and building of play dens, along with other play activities often went on well into the evening. We had to restrict the times due to some complaints from nearby elderly neighbours due to the noise level. The bungalows situated in fernheath road were resounding in hammering noise levels so I paid a visits to local pensioners and I apologized for the noise and gave them reassurance. Other problems on the site was that the bark strips on the fencing could easily be taken off by kids to enter the site when it was closed and unsupervised. There were numerous attempts made to resolve this including staff visits out of hours. The numbers of children attending had increased dramatically partly due to the excellent weather. This was apparent on Saturdays when many trips out took place, along with recreational games of cricket and rounder's on the co op grounds. Such activities involved hordes of children of all ages. The trips out in August to Bovington Camp Open Day and the camping expedition to south Wales were extremely successful ventures. The playground took an active part in the Bournemouth carnival as well as being the main group in the local Fernheath Community Festival held on the co op grounds. A variety of activities were organised both on the playing fields and in the sports pavilion. Whilst the children participated in painting competitions, den building contests in the playground and a barbecue. Now local parents and committee members were even more active locally in the playground and in fund raising initiatives. Julian Finch my former colleague from Skelmersdale adventure playground visited me with his wife and family and we spent some time together. Though it was sad to hear that the Skelmersdale adventure playgrounds wooden fence was burnt down and the playground was closed due to insufficient funds. The Development Corporation had withdrawn its funding and Barnardos were unable to fund the project alone. Julian is at present the Chief Executive of Bolton's (YMCA) Young Men's Christian Association. Whilst Malcolm King and Marten Kuiper from Cardiff established an adventure playground at Wrexham Wales in Cola Park.

On adventure playgrounds children learned and tested their own capabilities and from taking risks in climbing playing on wooden structures and swinging from Tarzan ropes, scampering up commando nets and jumping off of and landing safely from aerial runways. Here they developed their creativity through their imaginations. They learnt basic skills in building perhaps just flimsy dens or wooden structures initially but with practice and input support and encouragement from the play leaders these soon became more adept and imaginative and structurally sound. As they too became familiar with the tools and materials of the playground. They learnt physical skills through carrying a range of heavy materials of all shapes and sizes, materials such as wood, tin, rope bricks etc. Here children learned through their play by means of trial and error without the restraints of adults or health and safety controls. They learnt through self discipline and developed self confidence and empathy for others in their social grouping mixing with others of all ages and abilities. They became actively and physically fit. From urban inner cities, housing estates, rural country areas and new towns, child's play made its mark on both old and new communities. Influencing the lives of thousands of children since the very first play experiments were put into practice during the early post war years. The building of their many playground camps and dens in these pioneering days, was how many children learnt to co-operate and to share with one another. Often at first these dens were of flimsy constructions, often consisting of just no more than just four wooden pallet boards sides, plus a roof held together with just a few nails and a prayer. Gradually with construction experience, children became confident and adept adding extra rooms and ramps. Then as they became more skilful, adding sliding doors, or hinged trap doors, extensions and underground entrances and exits. The art of building became a matter of achievement both between competitive groups and within groups, leading to co-operation and assistance. Swaps of materials, with deals, became a common place. Such activities became an essential part of the day to day adventure playground environment of the kid's community. The actual building process became more of a need than the completion for once completed they soon became bored and often would destroy it and start again on another building project. Therefore fulfilling the term re creation or recreation.

Here the children learnt to control fire in a safe setting, to cook basic meals and to share the social setting of their fireside gatherings with others. In social dialogue to perhaps tell stories, sing songs, or just to confide their fears and share their concerns with their fellow peers and thus they became members of a community. Those who were adept at building, constructed elaborate dens storey's high with trap doors, secret entrances, slides and even brick fireplaces. Others were elaborately designed with carpeting interiors, or mattresses throughout with wind holes with curtains. Others were busy digging out large holes in the soil and lined them with wooden walls and a base of wood and carpeting, with sheets of tin roofing and wood structural supports. Whilst young girls were to be seen busily dressing up in a range of pretty dresses gathered from a box in the play hut with fancy bonnets and garlands of beads or necklaces. Many young children took rides in the elaborate wooden roundabout made from just a tire base and wooden duck boards lined and padded out with foam and carpeting. Others took responsibility for tending their very own garden plot or caring for the animals in the pets areas of rabbits, hamsters, goat etc. In future years within the play building others youths ran the disco unit which they had constructed themselves and offered regular evening sessions music pop . Some youths were in the office talking to the play workers maybe ordering the playgrounds own shirt with logo or perhaps booking their place on the next playground trip out or the forthcoming camping weekend. Others were busy gathering damaged pieces of wood into sacks to be delivered later to the elderly in the local neighbourhood like those on the firewood service list. Groups of children were busy outside of the hut on the playground, climbing the ladders of the tall wooden play structures all created from telegraph poles with high safe walkways made from shuttering boards. Others sliding down the lino safety surfaced slides onto safe play surfaces of bark, grass or sand below or playing chase games round the dens. Initially it was the cities that were to be the testing grounds for the adventure play ideals of those early advocates of play like Lady Allen. Here child's play was itself often limited to a great extent by the harsh surroundings of urbanization, busy streets and limited space. However there were certain advantages, like the availability of waste materials from the demolition of the bombed sites and vacant properties. Along with cash grants available from government community development projects and the (N.P.F.A) National Playing Fields Association itself. Junk playgrounds had begun to establish themselves as isolated experiments set up by enthusiastic local people whose only resource tended to be time, coupled with a passion for this form of children's play. Often the land available could only be used for a short time prior to new housing development. And as was often the case at the start there were often no grants to equip and run these projects. Adventure playgrounds provided a unique centre of support in the local community partly because they were able to cater to children of all ages. The under fives child care provision later attached to some adventure playgrounds in some ways made up for the shortage of day nursery provision. Activities taking place in adventure playgrounds also tended to strengthen the networking function to bring social groups together. From toddler groups to pensioners' tea parties and often these encouraged a supportive atmosphere where children undertook community service tasks such as wood deliveries to pensioners. While parents and local people would donate waste material or rally round when there was a crisis of any sort. The early adventure playgrounds were unique as they usually had only one leader and he had to rely on voluntary help with little funding. His main role was to be reliant in that of scrounging of materials. The advantage of the adventure Playground is mainly psychological: its direct human contact with people's emotions. The warden, or whatever he called himself then, has to live with the families in the neighbourhood. There are no convenient hours. In the early days we were often seen as anarchists or social activists due to our philosophy of freedom in play. These Inner city adventure playgrounds were usually established as a direct result or response to local public pressure. Here space was limited, unlike some of the new towns or housing development areas. Often the only choices for towns such as London, for development of adventure play sites was the old sparse bombed sites, demolition areas, railway sidings or areas not required or considered as being suitable for building of housing or commercial use. Thus so often the only sites offered for play was unfortunately not ideal, often situated next to busy roads or else with limited space and sparse with no trees or grass. Play facilities in the cities are in many aspects quite different in character from those based within more rural surroundings. Adventure playgrounds in the city can differ in character from others even just a short distance away.

*Youth workers with regular Martin Dibben and children at the
adventure playground summer 1984*

Back at the fernheath adventure playground, members of our
team of play workers visited Basingstoke play centre's courtesy
of Jack Lambert. All part of a short play course I organized, based
at the local West Howe Henry Brown Centre. The idea being to
counteract the isolation of play workers and to encourage mutual
support and development of child's play at a local level. There

were many group discussions and topics including an "Introduction" by Arthur Taylor, "What is child's play" by Wendy Chandler Bournemouth Pre School Play Association P.P.A" , Why adventure playgrounds" by Pat Kirkwood Regional Officer of the N.P.F.A. "Using waste materials" by Mary Crabtree of Poole Play Council, "First Aid" by Brenda White of St John's Ambulance Brigade and "The Future of play in Bournemouth" by Roger Browne Recreation Officer of Bournemouth Borough Council. and the N.P.F.A film "Children Waiting" was shown. We also covered such topics as "Involving the local community", "Teenagers on adventure playgrounds, "Contacts in the community" and "The holiday programme". One of our team of play leaders Geoff Meddle (who was originally from London's Cheswick's famous Women's Aid Refuge centre) was successfully interviewed for a post and appointed as leader of Southampton Adventure Playground. At this time Ian Fletcher had established "Make Children Happy". This was a children's charity which produced a play work newspaper "Its Child's Play". By the autumn the Fernheath adventure playground was well established, with its own constitution, courtesy of "Fair Plays" Sue Kearsley and grant from Manpower Services, (NPFA) National Playing Fields in 2019Association etc for staff funding. However by the late autumn I was suffering from tonsillitis and was advised to take time off work, shortly after I was dismissed. When I recovered from the illness I took the matter to an industrial tribunal at Southampton and after proving the case I was offered full compensation and an offer of reinstatement, which I declined. After I had left in 1977, the adventure playground continued to operate with Rob Whitty as leader for many months with voluntary support. Nigel Jones had left at the same time. The success of the Fernheath adventure playground helped in many ways to pave the way in the area for other play initiatives. Fernheath Playground still operates forty years after its formation. There has obviously been many changes of leadership over time at the Playground and many generations of children.

Patricia (Paddy) Williamson and Ted Taylor with members of Fernheath Play association and the children of the scheme 1975. Picture courtesy of Brian Keets.

THE PEOPLE WHO SHAPED CHILDRENS PLAY

The following is based on an article I wrote and was published for The play and playground magazine in 2019.

By the time I first arrived at N.P.F.A s Play Field house their play leadership department was well established. With Drummond Abernethy at the realm assisted by a team of retired military officers over a number of years and dignitaries such as Lord Luke, Capt Wicksteed, Capt Tony Way and Capt Forbes alongside Alan Curtis, Mary Nicholson and the former editor of Pen magazine.

Prominent Play Workers.

Pat Turner the former adventure playground leader, Pat Smythe at Notting Hill and Ed Burman Camden had now established play parks and 1oclock clubs in the London parks such as Holland Park and Battersea, along with holiday play schemes. Jumbo

Vines worked on play structures for Battersea and Lewisham. Whilst nationally Joe Benjamin and others, as at Birmingham Gene Peck at Sparkbrooke adventure playground and Mike Buckley of Birmingham and Camden London. Harry Shiers at Coronation road adventure Playgrounds Birmingham, Mint street and Walworth adventure playgrounds in London. Mike Buckley was one of the very first adventure playground leaders in London and was responsible for setting up the adventure playground after moving from Birmingham to Gospel Oak to work for Camden Council's social services. Janet Dalglish played a major role through 4 decades as adventure playground leader in London then as President of Fair Play for Children. Along with Pat Smthe and Francis Mc Lennon at Notting hill and Angel town adventure playgrounds. Matt Mc Guinn the folk singer was establishing adventure playgrounds at Glasgow. By the 1970s very many others followed. For instance at Stevenage Donne Buck was at Bandley hill adventure playground where adventure playgrounds were established at Chells,The Canyon,Pin Green and St Nicholas in this new town. With play workers such as Chris Nichols at the Canyon and Mike Fowler. Jack Lambert established an adventure playground at Welwyn garden city and later he wrote about in the Pengun publication "Adventmure Playgrounds" He later became Play officer at Basingstoke. Sue Townsend established adventure playgrounds in the city of London before leaving to write children's books along with Dorothy Whittaker becoming a International Volunteer. Helen Gush at Newport adventure playground left to marry a London probation officer. Tony Chilton at Blacon Chester,Harry Shiers,Bob Hughes at Haverhill Suffolk developed numerous adventure playgrounds and became well established figures in the play movement for many decades. Chris and John Winkley of St John's Wood Adventure playground. Also Jess Milne at Londons Kings Cross,St Johns wood adventure playgrounds before he worked at Sheffield.

Th e Adventure playground workers association and London adventure playground association had been established at Notting hill Adventure playground by Pat Smythe,Francis McLennon, Mike Buckley,Jim Jackson and Leo Jago. An

Institute of Play was established with a Diploma course at Thurrock run by Colin Mayne. Over the course of the 70s the N.P.F.A play leadership department employed experienced play workers as regional officers. Notably Mick Fitzmaurice and Alan Jenkins. These were followed by Nick Balmforth, Harry Shiers,Keith Cranwell,Bob Hughes,Rob Wheway,Tony Chilton, Bill McCullough, Frank King, Mike Halsey and Andrew Scott. With Nick eventually taking over Drummond's role on his retirement as Director of the Play leadership department. The (N.P.F.A) National Playing Fields Association published their guidelines on playground safety entitled "Towards a Safer Adventure Playground" written mainly Bill McCullough and Frank King and had a marked impact upon Adventure Playgrounds both then and in the future. During these years there were many national campaigns including the formation and establishment of "Fair Play for Children" led by the revs Trevor Huddleston Bishop of Stepney. The organisation was led in future years by people such as Donne Buck, Stephen Rennie,Sue Kearsley and then Janet Dalglish became its president for very many years. Other individuals who established play associations and operated schemes for decades included Patricia Williamson at Fernheath Bournemouth and Betty Pickerskill at Stevenage. Over the years Fraser Brown became a prominent name in child's play work after working on many adventure playgrounds including Runcorn. He worked on projects throughout the North with the North West play associaton as well as leisure services in Middlesborough before becoming the Reader in play work at Leeds University. Nottingham had numerous advrenture playground throughout the 70s notably at St Anns which was established by Roger Braybrooke.

Roger Braybrooke and kids on the St Anns adventure playground 1975

By the 1980s there was concerns of safety of conventional playing fields playgrounds or swing parks and a national campaign was successfully undertaken to improve safety standards on these unsupervised play favcilities. The body met at Playfield house and included representatives from all concerned

185

including those from safety on playgrounds Acton group. With Donne Buck at the fore front it was supported by TV celebrity Esther Rantzen and Paul Rose MP. Paul Bonel worked on numerous adventure playgrounds in London during this time and worked closely with N.P.F.A. Whilst Maynell the director of Maynel Games became prominent over the next 30 plus years. Stephen Rennie in recent years worked on many play projects and became senior lecturer in play work at Leeds University.

Over many decades Penny Wilson worked for the Play Association Tower Hamlets – PATH in the East End of London and at Chelsea Adventure Playground for the disabled. She was a member of the Play work Principles Scrutiny Group and condensed the work of Bob Hughes, Gordon Sturrock, and Mick Conway producing the Play work Principles. Penny continues to be a strong advocate for play both in the United Kingdom and in the United States.

Importance of Play – The Play work Principles

1.   All children and young people need to play. The impulse to play is innate. Play is a biological, psychological and social necessity , and is fundamental to the healthy development and well being of individuals and communities.

2.   Play is a process that is freely chosen, personally directed and intrinsically motivated. That is, children and young people determine and control the content and intent of their play, by following their own instincts, ideas and interests, in their own way for their own reasons.

3.   The prime focus and essence of play work is to support and facilitate the play process and this should inform the development of play policy, strategy, training and education.

4.   For play workers, the play process takes precedence and play workers act as advocates for play when engaging with adult led agendas

5. The role of the play worker is to support all children and young people in the creation of a space in which they can play.

6. The play worker's response to children and young people playing is based on a sound up to date knowledge of the play process , and reflective practise.

7. Play worker's recognise their own impact on the play space and also the impact of children and young people's play on the play worker.

8. Play workers choose an intervention style that enables children and young people to extend their play. All play worker intervention must balance risk with the developmental benefit and well being of children.

Wendy Russell has worked in Child's play for 4 decades on adventure playgrounds and their development. In recent years She **is a Senior Lecturer in Play and Play work at the University of Gloucestershire and a consultant on children's play and play work.**

CHAPTER TWELVE

MORE ADVENTURES IN CHILDS PLAY

Ray Wills chair and organiser with local children as an event operated by ACT Residents Association Bournemouth 2012.

Freedom to Play
Locked in their world of close circuit TV
reality life and crude imagery
far away from the streets of their play liberty
The jingles they play and the media tells lies
whilst their childhood is lost in their sadness and smiles
the thunder it roared and the prophets foretold
of days yet to be when childhood grew old

There were limbs on the trees and fields left to roam
but the candle was dimmed and their visions were closed
their masters and kin folk guided their dreams
with take away foods and horrific loud screams

There was food on the table and news on the spree
where doctrines and war crimes paraded for thee
the masters of visions crafted their dreams
with false words and logic no room for ice cream

The songs and the rhymes were lost in the maze
of corrupted lost childhoods in the latest whiz craze
the songsters were singing the same dulcet tones
with bleached hair and promises wrapped up in gold

The streets they were quiet no sounds of child's play
another dream over at the end of the day
whilst a comic gave rant and a poet he prayed
for a childhood forsaken and a vision waylaid.

Ray Wills

Dog Kennel Hill Adventure Playground East Dulwich Southwark London

This project was started by a group of local residents who formed a committee East Dulwich Play Association. The playground management committee consisted of local people and a BBC TV producer of children's Blue Peter programs. With the project coordinated by Des Palmer from the Southwark Council Social Services *In 1977 Stuart Russell a play worker who had been operating from Norwich play schemes and I were appointed. To establish a new Adventure playground at Dog Kennel Hill for the East Dulwich Play Association in London. Prior to us working together Stuart visited me in Poole Dorset and we became close friends.* Stuart had recently completed the Thurrock Diploma in Play Work course under the direction of its tutor Colin Mayne. We were to establish a new adventure playground on a really lovely site which was a large, undulating grassy woodland area, ideal for child's play. It was situated on the west edge of the extremely steep and busy Dog Kennel Hill. This was just above the King George playing fields, opposite to the large G.L.C Greater London Council housing estate and it backed onto a private sports members club, a gypsy site and tennis courts. Grant aid for the project came from Southwark Council and the (N.P.F.A) National Playing Fields Association. The license for the site was initially granted to the trustees of the play association by Southwark Borough Council for an initial period of 15 years. The application was made via the play association through Des Palmer their coordinator. Whilst at East Dulwich Adventure Playground I commuted daily to the playground from the Sandford housing co op near New Cross, Deptford, where I lived with Stuart and other professionals, teachers and students.

Stuart Russell and I worked initially in detached roles, visiting local schools, clubs, on the streets of the estate. Talking to groups or individual children, or with local residents and church groups. In this way building up a network of relationships with children and community leaders. It has always been seen as of great importance in the development of any new adventure playground that the first play leader appointed is able to have a period of time before actual work on the adventure playground site begins. As a period of time in which he or she gains contact with local children and community leaders and builds up a network of people and resources. In this way play leaders, have involved the children in the actual playground's development from the very start and the kids feel that the playground is truly theirs. Many play leaders have used this period of time to meet groups of kids in a variety of settings, such as school classrooms, youth clubs and on the streets. Or in less formal settings such as the local swing parks, in fact wherever children congregated in their free time. In such settings, the play leader was able to best relate to them and explain the plans of the new project. The kid's involvement in these early stages was paramount, with many relationships formed between the leader and groups of children, the future users of the play scheme. In this way by the time of the playgrounds official opening , the play leader had built up a nucleus of young people who were keen to be involved, making the task of acceptance that much easier. Two regional (N.P.F.A) National Playing Fields Association officers and former play leaders, who had their own views on the value of this arrangement, were Mick Fitzmaurice and Alan Jenkins. They remarked in their (N.P.F.A) National Playing Fields Association publication that, "it is our strong feeling that the first step in developing a permanent adventure playground, or play scheme should be the employment of a play leader".

We made regular visits to the local primary school where we talked to classes of pupils and ran picture and poem competitions to advertise the adventure playground and publicize its future opening. The play site itself was full of dangerous items, which had obviously been dumped or left from its earlier nursery days. With heavy brick rubble, glass, galvanized sheets of tin, huge oblong blocks of stone up to five feet in length, which were extremely heavy. All of which needed to be taken from the site before we could consider using the site for child's play. We therefore decided to have this as a project in which all of the local community could be actively involved. Involving local school groups, residents groups, play management committee, local police and children. In clearing the site of such dangerous materials. We approached the local gypsy camp and they were more than willing to help with removal of the heavier rubble providing a crane and a chain, other groups helped with the collection of rubbish, bottles and other rubbish and it was proven to be a very successful activity. With children, parents, schools, clubs and local groups all involved. Other projects involved the local school kids in poetry, art, competition, with the adventure playground being the theme. This was another way in which we were able to gain publicity for the adventure playgrounds future establishment and existence.

The Play Association itself ran a very successful craft fair event, which was held in the Dulwich village St Barnabus church hall. With over 47 stalls with live music was provided by the East Dulwich Heber Road School steel band. Stuart and I assisted on the day with sales of programmes on the doors. Over 200 people attended on a sunny summer's day, raising hundreds of pounds as well as free publicity for the playground through sales of programmes and posters. Dulwich village itself was in sharp contrast to the crowded East Dulwich housing estate. Here was where the local MP Margaret Thatcher's constituency home was of nicely laid our grassed areas suburbia quiet and select.

Des Palmer Secretary of East Dulwich Play Association took my collection of notes all of my detailed advice on the formation of new adventure playgrounds and he presented them at the newly formed (LAPA) London Adventure Playgrounds Association. I was aware of the work of Harry Shiers at that time who was a close friend of Stuarts. At that time Harry was working at adventure playgrounds in Mint Street Southwark and Blendon Row Walworth. In later years and throughout the 1980s Harry was based in Birmingham as Assistant Resources Officer and Adventure Playground Coordinator at Coronation Road Adventure Playground. Whilst Paul Vines (known affectionately as Jumbo) was busy designing play structures at Slade Gardens, Battersea and later at Honor Oak Adventure Playground Lewisham throughout the 1980s. One afternoon I bumped into Charles Rudd play leader on the street nearby who was working with street youths just a few yards from the playground. They were using a former brick air raid shelter as a club house.

The fencing of the playground remained of great concern with it being so close to the steep and dangerous dog kennel hill road. Directly opposite to the East Dulwich estate where the majority of local children lived. Children who were to use the adventure playground would have to cross the steep hill, with no crossing or patrol to enter the site. Initially the creation and construction of the fence itself became a big manual exercise, which took up a great deal of our time with members of the committee's assistance. Joining large sections of heavy tin sheeting together and constructing this fencing around the perimeter of the site, was a strenuous exercise in the hot weather. Stuart and I set to the designing of a plan of the proposed adventure playground site layout, including the position of the play hut, its services, access including entrances and exits for children and vehicles. The play structures area and others were planned including hard surface games areas, barbecue areas and children's den building areas. For the actual barbecue area construction we made good use of the 8 large heavy 6ftx2ft stones slabs which were already present on the site, these were ideal for the seating in a circular area. The initial, temporary hut was a tin shed, which was to be used for the storage of tools and play materials. There were plans afoot for a play hut building which were approved at a cost to the region of £25,000 when fully equipped, with the monies to be provided through an urban aid grant. The fencing was now constructed around the site, although I saw this as unsuitable and as a temporary measure, considering the public access problems, the narrow footpath between the playground fence and the steep dog kennel hill road. All of the various necessary projects were therefore undertaken prior to the actual day of the playgrounds opening, including the creation of soil steps cut out of the rise at the rear of site exit. However at this particular site sparsely of trees or grass was not the issue. For in many ways the actual size and environment was ideal, with its woodland, bushes and undulating grassy banks, it was in fact beautiful in many aspects with a natural layout compared to so many others sites I have encountered. Of all of the adventure playgrounds of which I have known, this site still remains my favourite with immense possibilities for all of the child's play needs to be met within one setting. My concerns over the issue of children's safety took me into direct conflicts of interest with members of the play association. I was anxious that the site had a strong concrete horizontal fence, as recommended by the (N.P.F.A) National Playing Fields Association This was particularly relevant with the dangers of the close proximity to the steep hazardous hill road and the children having no crossing from the nearby estate to the site and with no patrol or crossing of any description. Other people just wanted the site to be opened and operational for the school holidays. I felt it necessary to approach the local authority's safety officer who fully supported my concerns though was not in a position to go against his superiors. I had to therefore make a decision on principle and therefore gave in my notice, as I was not prepared to accept responsibility for any child being seriously injured, as a direct result of no correct fencing or safety patrol. I was to hear later of a child being tragically killed crossing Dog Kennel Hill which was the steepest road in the city of London. The structures weave in and out of woodland and some even incorporate trees. Dog Kennel adventure playground in East Dulwich operated until a fire in 1998 then for a short period it was run by Southwark council and is now back in the hands of the voluntary sector. It is now an award winning adventure playground.

Meanwhile in Dorset the fernheath adventure playground site now had its own permanent play building installed, with most of the work being undertaken by local people and pupils from Oakmead School on an education project called "operation lift off". They were involved in the removal of the changing rooms from the Victoria park playing fields in Bournemouth and erecting them at fernheath. The project was sponsored and awarded by the National Westminster Bank for their "Project Respond" successfully gained their coveted award.

At East Dulwich dog kennel hill adventure playground

At that time whilst working at East Dulwich and after I was living in Sanford housing co operative and was a member of their committee of The Society of Cooperative Dwellings Deptford London. Living just a stone throw from cold blow lane where the Millwall football team played. I was given the co op contact by an administrator of Kensington and Chelsea Play Association who knew me from previous years. I would come into daily contact with kids on the streets either from Deptford itself or from the nearby large woodpecker housing estate. Particularly around October and November when they were out collecting monies for their Guy Fawkes and fireworks collection as is traditional in the UK. At our social committee meeting in the co op I came up with the suggestion that the housing co-op should hold its own community bonfire and involve all members as well as children from the locality. This was approved and later I made contact with the many local kids as they were collecting monies for the traditional penny for the guy. I approached them and encouraged them to get involved with our community bonfire preparations. Bringing all of these various "penny for the guy" groups together under the umbrella of the Sanford committee. Thus the scene was set for a community bonfire and fireworks display to be held on the car park area at cold blow lane by the bridge. It was financed through the co op committee with fireworks donated through a contact of mine Andy Scott Play who was now a Play Organiser and was involved at Fair Play for Children. The students and teachers at the co- op volunteered for the evening with British Rail donating old railway line sleepers which we used for the base of the bonfire. The committee members all made cakes for the refreshments whilst all the local shops were approached and donated crisps, soft drinks and prizes for the Guy Fawkes competition. The local kids who I had befriended arrived with all their numerous home-made Guy Fawkes s and were active in building and preparing the bonfire with cardboard, paper and rubbish, whilst local dads delivered trucks full of wood. The entire street at Sanford walk turned out that evening, potatoes were roasted, sweets and cakes were readily eaten and soft drinks handed out with crisps along with prizes for best Guy in our Guy Fawkes competition. Over 80 children attended with local police and fire service all notified and the area was roped off and safety checked. The Adults present took responsibility for the fireworks displays and safety measures, with buckets of sand and water handy. The bonfire was extremely large, its heat lasted through the night and the embers were still there in the morning light. It was a real community bonfire the first in the area. Later at Christmas we organized a children's party, many of the local children were invited free, this was held in the woodpecker community centre at the woodpecker estate with a great many children present. This event was well supported and sponsored by the local social services department, with many of their children attending. I provided hundreds of balloons which the volunteers blew up and later released from a net. This was an exciting event. During the winter the BBC Panorama TV crew visited with Cliff Michelmore and filmed one of our Housing Co-op meetings for a special Panorama programme on housing issues.

Kimber Road Adventure playgrounds Wandsworth -London

In1978 following discussions with my friend and former colleague Wandsworth Play organiser Andy Scott. I was offered a post at various adventure playground sites for the summer period as a kind of trouble shooter. I was extremely interested and accepted his kind offer and worked as a casual adventure playground worker on two sites, during the summer. The main adventure playground at Kimber road, was sited within a park, close to a large Greater London council housing estate and just walking distance away from the main shopping centre. I was part of a team of play leaders who rebuilt the adventure playground and decorated the play hut, along with the play structures. The site had suffered over the years from drug-related problems, vandalism and poor leadership. The lady leader and our team of play staff, successfully built a new go-kart track around the site, created a barbecue area, along with slides and rope Tarzan swings. Whilst employed I attended the NPFA play leadership course ran by Andrew Scott at Goldsmiths College. I was to visit Andy in his flat around that time where I discovered his hobby was music and he now played drums in a local beat group.

Meanwhile at that time in Redbridge Diana Casswell and her husband the Reverend Peter Casswell, set about starting the first adventure playground specifically for children with disabilities outside of inner London. Forming ELHAP Adventure Playground Redbridge London IG8 From the start a body of

197

committed and experienced people joined the management committee to oversee its creation. ELHAP had taken over the site from Barnardo's in 1975 and by September 1976 negotiations had been completed with the charity. In 1977 it officially opened as a playground for disabled children. Within a short time of opening demand was such that a timetable of use had to be created to allow all the users to regularly visit. Set up by Drummond Abernethy, *who upon his retirement from (N.P.F.A) National Playing Fields Association in 1978 became its chair. A position he retained until ill health forced him to stand down in 1986, whilst he remained on the executive* committee until his death. A great deal of the success of ELHAP is attributed to him. Under his guidance E.L.H.A.P developed into a thriving playground. Drummond described E.L.H.A.P as the "the very best adventure playground for children with disabilities". The playground was set in four acres of an old farm; the walls of the farm buildings and traces of an old orchard remain. Two acres are dedicated to a play scape and the remainder left as a nature area with paths and benches. There is also a see-saw that can accommodate wheelchairs. "E.L.H.A.P.A changed its name to Kids Active and merged with another charity KIDS.

Meanwhile at my former playground at Balsall Heath Malvern street in Birmingham the artist Derek Horton had arrived from Hockley Port Adventure Playground Birmingham.(later in the early 80's John Dale was to be its Play leader).

Derek recounted those years. "I arrived in Balsall Heath in 1978 to work as a 'community artist' at the adventure playground on Malvern Street". In many accounts of the history of Balsall Heath, not least in its own website, the arrival of St Paul's marked some kind of 'year-zero' in self-organisation and community activism in the area. This is not the case, and, although what we knew then as "The Venture" on Malvern Street came under the St Paul's umbrella and expanded over the road to a city farm and a sports pitch, it was founded in 1969 by Balsall Heath Community Association, supported by the Cadbury Trust, with Ray Wills as the first play worker. Wills had previously worked with the pioneering Gene Pack, who, with funding from the Save the Children Fund, set up the Sparkbrook Adventure Playground in 1965, one of the first adventure playgrounds in the UK. 1965 was also the year of the first Sparkbrook Carnival, forerunner to the Balsall Heath Carnival, and also largely a product of Gene Pack's energies". "In the 1960's they became strongly influenced by the DIY counterculture emerging from California, and Lloyd Kahn's Dome book (1971) and Stewart Brand's Whole Earth Catalogues (1968-72) became virtual 'bibles' for many of us. Central to the philosophy was an ideological and ethical commitment to the idea of freedom, of play unhampered by adult rules, and to children's capability to engage in a kind of anarchic architecture. They were encouraged to use hand tools and even power tools themselves, with minimal training or intervention by adults to ensure their safety, in order to self-build an environment that they could determine and control." " My move was the adventure playground equivalent of moving from Los Angeles to Manhattan, the tiny parcel of land on Malvern Street forcing us to build upwards rather than outwards. By 1980, structures of scaffold planks and telegraph poles towered over the rooftop of the Railway Inn at the corner of Malvern Street and Clifton Road, in a way impossible to imagine in the over-regulated and health & safety-dominated world of 21st century recreational space". "In 1978 other people working with the kids at the Malvern venture then included Es Rosen, John Boulton and Monika Roberts, and later Ken Bonham who ran and expanded the city farm which was officially opened by the mayor of Birmingham in 1980 when the venture was part of St Paul's. It has constantly expanded to become the environmental education resource which it is today". - Derek Horton

Talacre Open Space Camden London

I applied for and took up the post of Sports, Play and Youth Co-coordinator- Talacre Action Group for this Camden Council of Social Services funded project in 1980. I was employed with a mandate to supervise their Play, youth and sports leaders and to co ordinate and develop sports, play and youth facilities in the neighbourhood. Talacre Action Group was a local voluntary body. The Open space has a rich history. It made Talacre Open

Space very unusual – because whilst most London parks were created by leaving open space and building around it. Talacre had occurred due to demolition of slum housing and both listening to and following local people's wishes. Lady Marjorie Allen had originally been involved with as its former Secretary. Before my appointment the previous co-coordinator of the Sports Play and Youth programmes had left the job after only a brief time and the committee were keen to see the scheme operate successfully. Unfortunately as I was soon to discover the scheme itself was full of internal problems .With low staff morale, pot smoking activity amongst staff, poor organisation and the unaccounted theft or loss of expensive play equipment, vehicle, cine projector and a number of go karts. After a short time in the post I decided that it was not really for me. Following initial discussions with Mike Buckley and a meet up on Parliament Hill with the head of play services in Camden. I made the decision to leave the position. I then gave my notice in following a meeting with the management group of the Talacre Action group at which I presented my report and my reasons for leaving. Around that time in 1980 Balsall heath Birmingham was shown on B.B.C TVs Pebble Mills magazines showcase education programme. It focused on a temporary adventure playground built by Balsall heath children in the grounds of the BBC centre at Sparkbrook (Pebble Mill).The programme was conducted under the professional guidance of my friend and colleague Nick Balmforth who was formerly the Regional officer of (N.P.F.A) National Playing Fields Association for the Midlands area and who became Director of the (N.P.F.A.) National Playing Fields Association when Drummond retired. Children from Balsall heath Birmingham were actively involved in the filming of this event. These series of programmes entitled "Jubilee Street Playgrounds" focused on the need for adventure playgrounds and play schemes nationally. A special edition of a B.B.C / N.P.F.A publication supported the programme. The (N.P.F.A) National Playing Fields Association published their guidelines on playground safety entitled "Towards a Safer Adventure Playground". This was written mainly by the now sadly deceased play workers Bill McCullough and Frank King. This publication was to have a marked impact upon Adventure Playgrounds both then and in the future. ("Fair Play" unfortunately has dissolved in recent years). Play England also had its origins via The National Voluntary Council for Children's Play (NVCCP).

In 1981–82 the Government gave more than £21 million to the Sports Council, plus local authorities urban aid programme funding for play-related projects received almost £10 million in funding. N.P.F.A service costs were about £¼ million a year largely raised through voluntary contributions, which was is in marked contrast to the Sports Council budget. N.P.F.A were facing a £150,000 deficit and had to drastically reduce its head office and regional staff. The government had stopped the funding for Fair Play for Children and had in 1983 created "Play board" as an umbrella organisation to co ordinate and plan children's play interests. Play Board, also referred to as The Association for Children's Play and Recreation coordinating work in children's play –never been achieved in the history of play organisations."It had a budget of over £800,000 and over twenty four times the resources of "Fair Play". The N.P.F.A regional structure was now dismantled and the newly formed Play Board aimed to coordinate 'play work' in its broadest sense. Through research, strengthening regional provision and to provide expertise to local play bodies. It had a mandate to formulate national standards for play work training and an accessible information service. It was to provide expertise to enable local bodies to create meaningful local policies for children's out-of-school leisure. This eventually over three years was to lead to a government move to seek a merger between Play board and The Sports Council. The Play board directors, however initially rejected this proposal and decided that rather than merge with the Sports Council they would close down Play board permanently. Nick Balmforth previously the West Midlands (N.P.F.A) National Playing Fields Associations Play Officer and future Director of NPFA and their Senior Communications Officer wrote to me then. Informing me that all of their staff had received redundancy notices.

I was now living in Dorset where Child's play was slow to develop, despite the county being the home of The Scout

Movement, the original home of A.S Neil's Summerhill free school at Lyme Regis, Homer Lanes- Shaftesbury's Little Commonwealth and the home of Lord Shaftesbury the children's reformer. As well as the birthplace and home of the William Barnes (Dorchester) the visionary and advocate of children's play. The Dorset county was also where Robert Louis Stevenson got his inspiration for Treasure Island whilst staying at his home in Westbourne and which over looked Poole quay. Enid Blyton who had lived in Swanage, used Dorset as her inspiration for all her children's adventure books, Corfe Castle in the Purbeck being the castle of adventure Carey Wareham the Dorset county education department established one of the very first children's school camps in the mid nineteen sixties.

Locally at East Stoke near Wareham in the early 1980s I organized their first community bonfire which has operated ever since, a venture supported by the Dorset county education departments kitchen facilities. Then by the mid eighties I co-ordinated the "Holicare" play schemes activities programme at the local Kingsleigh school in Kinson Bournemouth. A " Royal Wedding Party" in celebration of Prince Charles and Lady Diane's royal wedding was planned for our newly formed Kingsleigh school Parents Teachers Association (Friends of Kingsleigh). In the mid to late eighties I was a Manager for a local renovation scheme and coordinator of a regional gardening services for the elderly and disabled, operating from the Firs in Bournemouth. In 1986 Fernheath adventure playground was chosen for a Crime Prevention project by (N.A.C.R.O) National Association for the Care and Resettlement of Offenders and designated as a Public Health Action Area by the Dorset Health Authority. The Fernheath Playground site now included a preschool group, an after school club, a holiday play scheme and a multi-purpose play area.

Nationally by 1987 Play Board was gone. the centralised functions were gathered into a new unit with a greatly reduced budget. This was the National Children's Play and Recreation Unit (NCPRU) as part of the Sports Council. At that time I became involved with the national campaign for the "safety of children on playground's" campaign along with Donne Buck of "Fair Play For Children". This was an issue which I had been concerned with for many years previously. I had been corresponding with Charles Rudd of "The National Association of Recreation Leaders" of which I was a "Fellow" Member. Charles had been publicizing their concerns over conventional Playground Safety in their magazine Play Leader. With issues of the magazines displaying horrifying pictures of hazardous playground equipment with metal sticking out. It was then that I was approached by Rosemary Hamburger of the "Safety on Playgrounds Action Group", and responded with enthusiasm. I took on the role of Regional Officer for the campaign. Talking on local radio, gaining good front page editorial in the local press and gaining TV advertising space with public service announcements valued at twenty thousand pounds. I also wrote to the Design Council. The safety of children at play is now well recognized as essential in any future playground design, thanks to the national campaigns by (NPFA) 'The National Playing Field Associations' Safety Committee, 'R.O.S.P.A' and 'Safety on Playground Association'. For many years, since my initial involvement in play work, I have had extremely strong feelings regarding play facilities that were provided by local authorities for small children. These included the poor quality of play experiences that were provided in parks, recreation grounds and schools, with their tarmac and concrete surfaces, which such playgrounds provided .Adults always told the kids that this was what they the children really needed and wanted, for many decades. As a result, many countless kids have lost out on play opportunities and suffered from a range of accidents, caused in the main through poor planning and maintenance. I would continually bring the matter up at any opportunity to those in play work that would listen. Fortunately by the 1980's, others in the field of play work had similar concerns, with the formation of (NPFA) The National Playing Field Associations' own 'Safety on Playgrounds' Committee. Many others pressed those whom were responsible for British safety standards to look into the matter. Those in the media like Esther Rantzen and Bob Hughes spoke on the issue, and publicly voiced their concerns. As a result local authorities throughout the UK began to improve equipment and safety standards nationally. Within the county of Dorset, I had the subject aired on local radio, within the press and with support from 'Fair Play for Children'. Whilst I was acting in a voluntary capacity, as regional officer for the 'Safety on Playgrounds Association Action Group'. I continued to have regular telephone conversations and letters from the two spearheads of the campaign, Rosemary Hamburger and Patsie Lawler of the "Safety on Playgrounds Action group". Meanwhile Sue Kearsley of "Fair Play for Children", also kept me well informed of national play events. I had visits to my home from long time friend and former play worker Mike Halward now operating as a play consultant for his business Halward Associates. Mike was also an active member of the national "Fair Play" safety committee which met at (N.P.F.As) The National Playing Fields Association Playfield House. Since initially working under my supervision at Birmingham and Rogerstone Mike had managed numerous adventure playgrounds in London at Hammersmith and Westminster, developing play facilities in Kingston on Thames and as a South East Regional play officer for the N.P.F.A. At that time the loss of Urban Programme funding meant local authorities had to find the full costs of playgrounds in a period when all local authority expenditure was being cut. The national safety campaign was nationally coordinated and formally launched by "Fair Play for Children" in June of 1988. The British Standards Institute publicized new standards of play equipment and the issue was raised in the House of Commons. It was recommended that the Department of the Environment take a lead in improving standards on fixed equipment. A press conference was held at the House of Commons and chaired by Paul Rose M.P, whilst the campaign itself was launched through a Fair Play publication booklet, entitled "Danger's in the Playground," with Fair Play mobilizing support for the campaign itself. The issue remained a public concern for many years, I ran articles in the local press. Television celebrity Esther Rantzen ran a very successful TV campaign, and a voluntary code was introduced, for all local authorities, which has been adhered to. Much of this was due to the new safety standards set by the Institute and the continuing work of groups over the years like R.O.S.P.A, N.P.F.A, The

Safety Council and Fair Play For Children. Measures were taken to ensure the safety guidelines for play equipment was enforced this by numerous recommendations and these included-No sharp points or edges; Gaps must measure less than 3.5 inch or not more than 9 inch. Equipment more than 30inches high must be at least 9 foot apart. Such laws have helped prevent many dangers and accidents in playgrounds however playground designers still met with the challenge of making playgrounds fun for children whilst still making them safe and legal.

By the end of the decade things had changed considerably "The 1989 Children's Act development of Child Protection Policy meant that the free "come and go" access, on which the adventure playground ethos rested, was more formally monitored with tighter control over children's use of the provision. In 1990 children's play was returned back to the offices of (N.P.F.A) National Playing Fields Association thus adventure play now no longer had a credible national lobby to protect its interests.

L.A.P.A became known as Playlink and H.A.P.A became known as KidsActive before they both were disbanded.

At this time I was assisting with "Age Concern" Bournemouth swing boats rides event for children in the Bournemouth pleasure gardens An event which was mentioned in the Guinness Book of Records for its record numbers of children using the swing boats.

Locally in Dorset in 1993 the Dorset Child Care Clubs "Work N Play" initiative, was launched offering play opportunities, including art and craft, games, sports and drama. I attended their training days and the workshop at Poole whilst assisting Carole Powell the Play Manager based at the West Howe play scheme in Bournemouth in 1996.Compiling a resource pack on After school clubs for Dorset Care Trust. The Trust had run successful children's activity programmes alongside the county youth work programme, at numerous centre's in the county. At the time I visited the Fernheath Adventure Playground whilst I was assisting Carole Powell. I had some regular discussions with the Alan Marsh the leader of the adventure playground who was having difficulties with staffing and with meeting the new government standards of child care regulations which was now required. However the success of the adventure playground continued with the help of funds from the local authority and various charities and "The lottery fund". As part my training in management I compiled preparations document for the establishment of the new "Flippers Day Nursery" for Poole College Parkstone Poole. At the time of writing the Fernheath playground at Bournemouth has now been officially operating for 38 years, this is quite amazing for a town with an image of conservatism. It now also has a very successful additional supervised mothers and toddlers group which continues to operate daily and throughout school holidays, along with the councils holiday play schemes programmes on the co- op playing fields at Fern-heath Road, West Howe, Bournemouth. By 1998 with the launch of the "National Childcare Strategy", this placed the emphasis on the care of the child, undertaking purposeful play activities, as a paid "out-of-school" service which required that children be registered with a playground and only allowed to leave under strict supervision of a carer. This has created a situation on some adventure playgrounds where one group of children are "open access" and free to leave and return to the playground as they wish. Alongside children who cannot leave without a recognised carer – creating two types playground user. "Kids Club Network" evolved from "The National Out Of School Alliance".

At the end of the 1990s in London a utility company was digging a large tunnel to take huge power cables from St John's Wood to Hackney. The company asked if it could dig a shaft in a corner of the space, if it agreed to fill it in later. The company offered one and a half million pounds in compensation. Camden Council agreed. With the money, under pressure from local people who supported the space, Camden set about developing Talacre Open Space to its full potential. Workmen came to put up perimeter railings with gates. Gardeners arrived to plant flowerbeds and re-landscape the open areas. There was a new children's play area, and floodlit sports pitches. At local residents request the name was changed to Talacre Gardens. With the help of the architect

Cedric Price, Inter Action built Talacre Centre, the UK's first purpose-built community arts centre located next to the Talacre Open Space. Cedric Price's old building was demolished in 2002, and by 2003 a smart new sports centre was in place, surrounded by floodlit sports pitches and flower beds with wide green lawns.

In recent years very many adventure playgrounds in the UK are gone such as at Wandsworth London. Although others have re emerged and a few new ones too. Though throughout the uk there are around 150 at the last count compared to 500 in their heyday.

Locally in Dorset in more recent years the Bournemouth Council continues to operate their very successful holiday play schemes programme, sites throughout the town. Whilst numerous play clubs and after school clubs also flourished throughout the county, along with church run holiday play activity programmes. As well as the more traditional guides, scouts and associated activities. The Bournemouth Y.M.C.A, provides an extensive play programme each year. Carey schools camp has now expanded its resources and is an outdoor education resource centre. It was noticeable that by 2005 the pleasure gardens Bournemouth's central show-piece and tourist attraction, was operating regular supervised children's games on the grassed areas for small children, throughout the summer season. Bournemouth Borough Council continues to operate its various play programmes which are now called Boredom Busters and operate throughout Bournemouth in the school holidays. Numerous other play schemes, out of school clubs, camps, adventure centres and city farms flourished throughout the county. In recent years until 2015 I had lived for many years just a stone's throw away from the Fernheath Adventure playground in Turbary Park Avenue, close to Turbary common which is now a nature reserve. For a number of recent years I was socially active there chairing a residents group "ACT" successfully campaigned for a pelican road crossing on the busy Turbary park avenues mile stretch of road which divided West Howe and Wallisdown communities. I was also involved with "Heath Watch" assisting Dot Donworth in reforming the local nature group on the common lands of Turbary.

In 2019 I was approached by Chris Poolman to be involved in a historical play project covering the history of play in Birmingham and was interviewed in Dorset providing a history of my time in Birmingham result of this was the Project. Which is available to read and hear online.

A new project 'Let Us Play', an investigation of the 'state of play' today. This involves the collation of an archive of material to capture the Birmingham adventure playground movement of the 1960-1980's (funded by The National Lottery Heritage Fund). This will be followed by a wider 'live period' of events and exhibitions in 2021/22.

The History of the Adventure Playground Movement in Birmingham.

The National Lottery Heritage Fund funded this project which has explored the history of the Adventure Playground movement in Birmingham, specifically to look at three lost or 'ghost' adventure playground sites that emerged in the post-war period (Balsall Heath, Sparkbrook & Handsworth) and one contemporary site (Meriden, Chelmsley Wood).Groups undertook oral history training and conducted interviews with people connected to the playgrounds. We have also been collecting archive material relating to the wider adventure playground movement in Birmingham. The oral histories and archive material will be presented in 2021 as part of a series of exhibitions and a publication.

The first 13 of these interviews are now available online :

I have also in recent years been involved in operating a Facebook page THE INTERNATIONAL HISTORY OF CHILDS PLAY a page which I had created with access to thousands of items on play topics.

Ray Wills with local Bournemouth MP and members of ACT community resident action group Margaret Sunderani,Dot Donworth. Receiving an award by local community and Bournemouth Borough council for his community work in Bournemouth

ACKNOWLEDGEMENTS

This publications includes art illustrations courtesy of Dawn Jeanette Grant Harrison. Along with a variety of superb photos of numerous adventure playgrounds and people. Courtesy of Donne Buck and the Museum of Childhood at Victioria and Albert Museum in London. Geoff Gaisford Sparkbrook adventure playground Birmingham.

SUMMARY

"I loved giving children a space where they could just be children, where they could try and fail without being judged or assessed." Claire Griffiths - Manager, The Land.

In the past twelve chapters I have attempted to provide my account of a history of play provision in the UK. This is my own personal account so therefore it may well differ from others who have researched the subject or have their own personal recollections to draw upon. Their accounts will no doubt obviously differ from mine. Within this chapter I will be drawing upon these personal recollections and research to present a summary of my account. I have purposely tried to stay clear of abstract play theories or philosophical insights to try to keep it practical down to earth and presenting it as a personal story wherever possible. I did not intend this book for just social scientists, academics or so called play experts. Because the real experts of course are the children. the play needs of our children remain basically the same' in our present age, when compared to those children of previous generations. Modern day children have however, in many areas, become more sophisticated and have matured that much earlier than the children of yester years. From an age of 5 to 8 years they need to explore and to experience a variety of energetic pastimes of short periods. To play alone by themselves and with others as part of a group environment. To identify with other children, to respond to rhythmic sounds. To be able to make choices, rules and to share experiences and to co-operate in play and to organise their own play times. Later in middle childhood of say 9 to 11 years of age they need to engage in more strenuous activities with elements of roughness, to enjoy their roles as boys and girls. To engage in single gender as well as mixed gender activities and to participate in a wide range of activities with a wide range of play material .Children need to succeed in co-operative play that provides individual satisfaction, to plan, lead and to check their progress. To belong to peer groups and to gain the respect and approval of others. From adolescence they need to develop skills and co-ordination, activities which do not draw attention and to their own self awkwardness, as well as to participate in some activities in separate groups and also some together. To belong to various groups and to plan and develop their own individual activities. To choose such activities, to be leaders and to create their own games as well as to evaluate progress.

Adventure play today maybe not the same or identical to adventure play at Emdrup in 1943 and modern sites do not often look as unkempt as play workers Bertelsen's first junk playground. But these ideas continue to inspire adults to think seriously about children's play and how best to support opportunities for such play provision. This is a testament to the strength of the philosophical, theoretical, social and political values that can still be found on the adventure playground. Today there an estimated one thousand adventure playgrounds in Europe alone, largely in Denmark, Switzerland, France, Germany, The Netherlands, and in England. In Germany alone there are some 400 adventure playgrounds. Japan has a significant number of adventure playgrounds as well. Adventure playgrounds in cities like London continue to operate very successfully. At one time the London borough of Islington boasted a dozen adventure playgrounds many of which gained awards for excellence. Such playgrounds are a hallmark of the best of British. Inventive, creative, adventurous, charming and energetic to the end.

Adventure playgrounds catered for such adventurous kids who required adventure activities such as those that they formerly had access to in their secret waste ground hideouts and on the common grounds.

Since their initial presence in the field of play provision there have been numerous analysis and theories of what constitutes an adventure playground. These have ranged from an antidote or response to juvenile delinquency, outlets for Child's stresses and a way to channel their destructive energies into constructive activity. Play was stressed as being essential to a Child's development, social, mental, physical and creative etc. From the early theories of play worker Leo Jago the need for child to destroy and rebuild is a continual process, create, recreation. Later came the educational values of Child's play which evolved into preschool and into the child's daily school provision. Then there were the anarchists of the free play movement such as A.S Neil etc, the pioneers advocates of junk play like Paneth, Lady Allen. Marie Paneth and Drummond Abernethy. Then the early adventure playground pioneers like H.S Turner, Donne Buck, Joe Benjamin and Jack Lambert. Then ultimately the social interaction and social integration on the community orientated adventure playgrounds. Here it was where all sectors of the community were involved and provided or catered for. The adventure playground of the earlier junk site now became a creative construction site of den building and often elaborate engineering though on a simple scale. The use of tools on playgrounds was encouraged children's skills were developed in carpentry and engineering then came the development of the play structures aspect from telegraph poles, railway sleepers, construction site beams, shuttering boards etc. Play workers then had to adapt and were trained in play structure building as well as social and community work, along with the psychology of play etc. Then the adventure playground became part of the social welfare field with liaison with social, education and leisure services. Due to the playgrounds development of preschool play, nursery, youth section, senior citizens group, disabled provision, parents groups etc were all within its building. Then the adventure playgrounds emphasis became on the importance of community involvement of all ages disabilities and abilities. It was a social setting a family catering for everyone and encouraging community interaction. Such playgrounds blossomed with the involvement of parent support groups, local welfare groups and community organization.

Then came the cuts in services by central governments and the loss of funds from various governments guanos which were lost. Then the interpretation of the "Health and safety Act" became a concern nationally and gave local authorities an opportunity to question the place of what they considered to be untidy and messy sites. Where children used a range of tools and materials that the authorities saw as being potentially dangerous. At the same time there was public campaigns such as "stranger danger" issues. All campaigns which many local authorities were concerned with and as a result more playgrounds were lost in the process by the result of these political and public concerns. With playgrounds becoming seen as unsafe or no longer needed and Peter Kemp, writing in The Times, remarked that children's play in England was a mess. He wrote, "Whether one looks at [children's play] from the point of view of parents or children, the practitioners in the field or the social theorist in an office, play is an essential part of a growing child's environment. Where, then, has play stood within government! The answer is 'all over the place'". He went on to list six government departments that had responsibility for some aspect of children's play arguing that there should be a single point of responsibility. However, it took until 2006 to see the establishment of Play England.

Recently the theories of Child's play in adventure playgrounds have recognized the "risk factor importance in Child's development". Along with the emphasis value of "loose parts" in play and this has become the current theme for the present need and upsurge in interest with the need for more adventure playgrounds for today's children. Adventure challenges and taking risks is an essential part of growing up: it is the way that children learn about themselves and the world around them. Adventure playgrounds provide children with the opportunity to take adventurous risks, safe in the knowledge that professional supportive help is there in the person of the play enabler if needed. There are literally hundreds of adventure playgrounds in the UK providing school-aged children with opportunities to play that are difficult to find elsewhere in our busy, urban environment. Fenced and secure, adventure playgrounds are often oases of nature in the middle of neighbourhoods. Typically, the majority of adventure playgrounds are open access: there's no charge to come in (though some have had to introduce charges to make ends meet)Here children are free to come and go as they please - after school, at weekends and during school holidays.

As child's play grew in influence particularly amongst the authorities and the planners. It was soon to become apparent that changes were necessary in the actual construction, locations and styles of provision. The log styled type of community adventure playgrounds of the 1970's era, which became so popular in the new towns housing development areas soon replaced the early junk adventure playgrounds. This primarily was due to specific public concerns relating to safety standards, the height of play structures, dangers of falls. Plus daily use by children of what were considered by many as flimsy structures and the child use of dangerous tools. The majority of Adventure playground now conduct regular risks assessments to ensure their feasibility. The adventurous activities like the Tarzan rope swings, the walkways, aerial runways, commando nets, and along with the towering climbing structures. All which could involve the children not only in using them, but also in their construction. The play activities which proved to be the most popular in the holiday schemes, such as traditional sports and games, were, football, cricket, shanty, table tennis, rounder's, snooker and darts. These were team games, although these were supported by the favourite playground group games such as chase, stuck in the mud, oranges and lemons; along with the usual traditional campfire sing along games, popular with scouts, guides and other groups. These various ranges of activities and play pursuits were all on the adventure playground fringes and could easily be included along with art, craft, music, cooking, camping and informal unstructured, den or camp building pursuits, of bonfires, digging, sand castle building, barbecues and similar unconventional pursuits. To these, one could add richness, by introducing an unlimited variety and number of new attractions within the adventure playgrounds own layout and design, such as a toddlers play area, specially constructed wooden roundabouts. Totem poles, pets area, bicycle racks, tool shed, storage area for play materials and timber, a youth section, football leagues, excursions out, visitors, specialized activities, candle making sessions and film-making activities. The list is endless and changes with the times and fashions. Unsupervised play provision

The need for special play places for all children, has resulted in town planners taking child's play into account with the provision of play spaces, toddler play space and conventional unsupervised playgrounds within housing estates. These were built professionally and situated close to their own homes and in their communities. Although these were without leadership, these were attractive colourful areas, though problems evolved over the years with vandalism, poor maintenance and safety issues being prominent. With the dangers of falls, onto tarmac or concrete these became a real problem. Then due to a great deal of much public concern safety surfaces became a necessity. Though present times demand fresh initiatives in play provision. Within the park play areas and play spaces that are scattered throughout the UK are the play spaces specifically designed for use by small children, with their log type effects, poles, ladders slides and rope walks. Many attractively coloured and with safety designed play surfaces, of sand, bark or rubber matting. Although these are in themselves vast improvement from the original tarmac and concrete playgrounds surfaces of the past with their dangerous metal ironmongery and wood equipment which once were the child's only play settings. Though there are now concerns over the rubber matting which heats in the summer and is felt to cause more serious injuries than bark or sand. The former play areas of static park playground equipment had been responsible decades earlier for thousands of injuries to children. Along with the foreboding school yard playgrounds which were bare, bleak and unimaginative places. This is one area however where children's play needs are yet to be fully met, School building which are still often not used sufficiently during weekends and school holidays. As adults many of us can no doubt recall the lonely harsh concrete or tarmac playgrounds of our school days. Where we were often shut out on cold wintry days to find our own pastimes, such as in rope games, rhyming slang, card flicks, marbles, jacks, yo-yos, spinning tops, hop scotch, elastics jumps, hula hoops, chase, leap frog or football.

It is no wonder that so many of our children have seen school as being anti social a threat. Losing interest in education at an early age. The playtimes of the school playground could well be a major extension of the school learning experience, if permitted to fulfil the children's own expectations. I am of the opinion that the child's school community should be a total social educational experience where the child is encouraged to play out his or her fantasies, imaginations. In a secure friendly and supervised play environment, along sides the more structured lessons. This is one area, which needs to be looked at seriously, as we go forward to the new millennium and prepare our children for fresh challenges and opportunities.

With the growth of leisure, 'Theme Parks', pleasure centres and amusement centres, have all mushroomed throughout country areas of the UK with their own distinctive style. These areas of play are all commercially packaged to meet the needs of a modern day mobile family yet provide little in the way of imaginative challenging or adventure risk play. There is also the ultimate Pleasure Park; 'Disney World', the nearest being located in France, largely based on the American popcorn, fantasy character world. The vast majority of these facilities still remain outside the financial reach of the majority of children in the U.K. Alongside the growth of the holiday packages, such as the former Butlin style family holiday camps of a previous decade with their own distinctive so called adventure play areas, crèches, nurseries, play clubs and activity clubs for children. So it is that play provision in its many forms and guises, is also deemed to be catered for within the holiday package industry. Any kind of playground which disturbs, or reduces, the role of imagination and makes the child more passive, more the recipient of someone else's imagination, may look nice, may be clean, may be safe, may be healthy - but it just cannot satisfy the fundamental need which play is all about. The need for some element of challenge or risk with objects which can be moved around by the child. *The term Adventure Playground is used as a generalization so often now. Thrown about by the general public t*o describe a wide range of commercial provision such as theme parks, holiday centre's etc. All such claims are erroneous to say the least in that they harm the original concept of Adventure Playgrounds. *Whilst the true Adventure Playgrounds are in fact none of these but areas of land set aside in a neighbourhood where local children* *have free access to play structures, play facilities indoors and out which are supervised by trained play staff. Within these sites the children are encouraged to take risks through means of a wide variety of play pursuits, aerial runways, slides, walkways, commando nets, etc. Here they are able to be actively involved in construction work themselves with use of tools and materials under guidance and supervision. These schemes are neighbourhood orientated with local parent's management committees and fund raising initiatives. A variety of activities can be planned including outings; social activities, play activities and community events. Each site can include possibilities such as gardening, pet's areas, nursery areas and youth sections, as well as barbecue areas . There is no limit to the range and variety of activities and functions on an adventure playground. Its development and its content depend to a great extent on the imagination of its users and the empathy of its leaders and staff. An Adventure Playground is a Community of children, with supporting play workers and parents involved in sharing and enjoying all the fruits of the play experience.*

Although the (false) unmanned, unsupervised, adventure playground concept is so often portrayed today with the name "Adventure Playground". With its variety of heavy weight unsupervised wooden, or plastic styles, walkways, towers, runways, slides, commando nets and their sandy safe surfaces. However, such facilities remain a poor substitute for the supervised play leadership, community based adventure playgrounds which we operated. With the former building creative aspects and activities organization and the active participation of the children.

The modern package so falsely called adventure playgrounds with their unsupervised facilities being only a minor substitute for the active, involved, all ages, interests centre, with supervision. Though in many ways it is truly a compliment to the original adventure playground ideal, that it has been so sweetly imitated on a small scale.

For adventure playgrounds to be truly successful, they have to provide for the total individual and groups. The construction of the adventure playgrounds with their large wooden climbing structures, walkway towers, forts, rope swings and aerial runways, involved the leaders and play staff in a great deal of heavy manual work. Trenches had to be dug out with holes large enough to support the telegraph poles and railway sleepers obtained from railway sidings. There were wooden support beams, shuttering boards, wooden duckboard/palettes, forestry logs and strips of four by two. Along with an endless number and variety of wood shapes, car tires, lorry tires, ropes nets and tackle, which when constructed stretched high into the sky. Ladders were constructed, along with wooden based slides for the younger children. Here there were wooden platforms, with rope swings to swing from, rope commando nets to climb, as well as rope Tarzan swing tires amongst an assortment of towers that led to forts. Along with a maze of climbing apparatus all towering high above ground level. The manual work involved was at times tiring, with the regular use of heavy good strong tools. These tools included hammers, saws, bow saws, tenon saws, crowbars, spades and shovels. Along with a vast variety and quantity of strong nails, bolts, rope and tackle; these were all most essential. All of the timber had to be checked regularly for strength and durability as well as safety, along with any fraying lengths of rope. Checks also had to be made regularly to ensure that the play structures were always safe and strong and were always safe to use for the purpose intended. Play leaders were always aware of the need for regular inspections of the adventure playground, to ensure that there were few real hazards. Hazards to avoid such as when a child would walk onto a protruding nail, or fall against a broken or damaged piece of splintered timber. The manual construction work could also include the play staff being involved in the building of the playground boundary fence, or in the initial construction of the play hut, or play building itself. Along with the creation of play mounds which were constructed using topsoil over a brick base. Children were obviously fully involved in all these activities particularly the older boys. Good leverage, rigid support, along with strength flexibility and weight of timber, were all matters to be considered in the actual building of the play structures. The variety of wood and timber was crucial, only good solid timber was used and such timber was checked for protruding nails, damaged areas and worn sections, which all had to be either replaced or strengthened regularly. Areas had to be adequately prepared for such work with sound foundations. Depth of supports was vital and treated with wood preserver, the use of concrete or cement was avoided at all times as this split wooden base and caused structural damage and danger. The size of nails and bolts, as well as their quality was checked and the range and quality of tools used for the best construction work was always the best. These included a variety of saws , planes, bolt cutters, claw hammers, crow bars, chains, tackle ropes and commando nets. Places set aside for storage of timber deliveries were essential, as was good access for swift deliveries, away from the actual children's play areas and near, of close proximity to entrances and exits. The construction of the play structures was never totally completed, with additional work on extensions and then finally with creative artwork, using paint to ensure that the play structures were all attractive, with a variety of colours and designs.

Although some of the hopes dreams and aspirations of the early pioneering play workers have to some extent been met since the early days, when organised play was in its infancy. Though it is still a sad fact of reality that the total picture nationally is still that of piecemeal play provision nationally and internationally. Due to a variety of factors, including lack of political persuasion, influence, adequate finance or space and suitable facilities. Although there has been certain growth areas, such as that of national safety standards and the maintenance of conventional play equipment along with the provision of safety surfaces. Nursery centres, play- groups, play schemes and many of the new developing out of school clubs, are still active. Whilst there are still adventure playgrounds and play centres which have survived and have adapted. Such as at Paddy Williamson's Fernheath in Bournemouth, Stevenage Pin Green or East Dulwich Dog Kennel Hill London. Play people have worked in vast varieties of settings. Bob Hughes built his first playground within four high grass banked walls, at Haverhill in Suffolk.

Brian Shaw operated on a small triangular piece of wasteland, on the Triangle at the Oval in Kennington London. Whilst Helen Gush ran her adventure site adjacent to a railway siding, at Newport Gwent in South Wales. Others have been more fortunate to operate within huge wooded canyons, like my colleague Chris Nichols at the Canyon Stevenage. Julian Finch first site was at the Delphs in a woodland area of Skelmersdale (Lancs.). Examples of these sites included parks and playing fields at Fernheath in Bournemouth, or a former Dickensian workhouse site at Mint Street (London) and a former garden nursery site at Dog Kennel Hill East Dulwich (London) where Stuart Russell and I worked. Other adventure playgrounds were situated on just a small area of land, such as opposite a London hospital in Fulham, or on a bombed site at Sparkbrook Birmingham, which Gene Peck led. The ranges of sites were versatile and extraordinary. Where anything is possible given the right people, children and local neighbourhood and where if it does happen successfully, this breeds other successes, in other communities as ideas are exchanged and taken onboard. I was fortunate to be actively involved in the movement during its most formative years. I worked alongside voluntary bodies as well as local authorities, development corporations and national charities, within inner cities, as well as rural and new town communities over a 30-year period.

As a play leader, I was prepared to take part in all of their energetic activities, sharing the play experiences of the children and for myself to find pleasure from being involved, as well as watching their enjoyment of play. Whilst the girls were more prepared to accept the social rules associated with the playing of games, boys demanded the space to show off their boisterous energetic natures. Many games provided channels for such outlets, where physical contact and aggression were the essential ingredients of the game at hand, such as football kick-about and other similar physical team pursuits. The play leader has to be aware of such needs, to ensure that there were opportunities for expression in many forms within the group and during the activities of child's play.

The relationships with so many children on adventure playgrounds and play schemes over the years had brought me into contact with literally thousands of children. Children of all ages and abilities. I always tried not to lead despite the term leader, although in many ways I had to instigate a vast variety of group games and chants which I gathered throughout the UK. This contact with kids often as young people as young as 2 and as old as 20 meant I had to be adaptable and approachable, versatile and energetic. I was lucky in that respect that children took to me easily it was just one of those things I guess. Being always surrounded by groups of kids many whom wanted to have shoulder rides, leg and wings or swings. So often demanding, small children clinging to me, though on the adventure playgrounds we provided so much variety of fun things to do to keep them all busy. Older youths would want to talk more or take part in more roustabout activities. Many would confide in me with their relationship boyfriend/girlfriend problems or in run in with the law and I would attend the court to speak up for them. Over the years I took many children away to Dorset on short breaks or arranged swop addresses holidays with families in Dorset and their homes. Children from Birmingham, including Margaret Carey, Eugene Donnelly, the Warren boys, Joy Henry, Christopher Pritchard from South Wales and Julia from Stevenage. Many of them still recall those visits in great detail.

Children from all social backgrounds were involved on the playground, including ethnic children and even those young people who were regarded as being un club able. These were often the adventure playgrounds greatest success. Play work across the United Kingdom has developed and survived since those early days principally because of the sheer strength of will of groups of play workers supporters and the networking structures they developed.

Children's playtime's have always adapted to the historical environment, with many of their street rhymes and chants told of social times, or circumstances, wars, political decisions, plagues, laws, kings, queens. politicians and even film or pop stars. Many of these rhymes are passed down from generation to generation,

222

or altered to suit changing styles as recorded by the Opies. These range from rhyming slang games to chase games and can include a range of activities such as the building of camps, tree houses and underground dens. To the more impromptu games of football, rounder's, cricket and ad hoc unsupervised activities, though with set standards, laws, rules, procedures, or rituals. Child's play itself can be impromptu with no adult present, as in the case of the activities, games and pursuits of children on the school playgrounds waste ground alleyways and common lands. Here children have themselves devised numerous pastimes. Then there are the play activities, which are supervised by Adults, with leadership or recreational skills; these are organized either at schools, clubs or similar organizations. These can be sports, art and craft, or involving children in more physical skills. Here there is an emphasis on team spirit, teamwork and competitiveness. Somewhere in between these two distinct areas of play is to be found the play work, or play with leadership disciplines, ranging from pre-school play groups, holiday play schemes, after school clubs to the more adventurous unstructured adventure playground, or play park. There are however sharp distinctions between play schemes and adventure play disciplines, with adventure play having a freer atmosphere. Being less competitive and more community based and with a stronger emphasis on the individual child, whatever their social background. Here there is an emphasis on strong links with other local community leaders and with an emphasis on physical structures of play, such as climbing forts and aerial runways. A more physical environment for the children to climb, slide and to develop at their own individual pace. There are of course the various crazes, or fashions which have made their impressions over the years in the child's own play world, such as the penny-farthing bicycles, hoops, go-carts, cock horses, spinning tops, yo-yo's, marbles, dolls, skateboards and roller skates; the list is endless. It is important that children's play should be recognized, as a child's right and in particular that specific places are set aside for children's playgrounds. Children need to play whenever and wherever they are, to feel safe and secure, within their own neighbourhoods. They need to be encouraged to use such play facilities, with practical use, safety and free movement. Places whereby parents could both, bring, monitor and observe their children, through interaction with other children. Attractive places within pleasant environments situated within each neighbourhood. So that play itself can develop and become a truly social and educational experience for all children, despite their own individual circumstances, or environments.

It has long been recognised that all children need variety in their play and access to a wide range of play activities. For them their play is their most serious occupation, often exuberant, yet with periods of intense absorption. Play for children is a most serious pastime, often requiring intense involvement, pre-occupation, patience and creatively. All bonded together with fun, gaiety, amusement and drama. Once they become involved in play, the adults; conception of time by the clock no longer exists and is no longer relevant to the child's world of playtime. Their play exists within a world of make believe and of that which the psychologist Abraham Maslow, defined as ;"The Now Experience". To the child all other distractions are not important, for once involved in these intense occupations they quickly become oblivious to the grown up calls of dinner time, or similar adult interruptions.

There are limited situations where the child's freedom and self discipline is allowed to flow and develop, where they can indulge safely in child plays own adventurous and imaginative pursuits. Places where they are able to share with their peers in fun and spontaneity, self-discovery and inventiveness, as is their right. All of this was to some extent freely available before the loss of their natural play space of wastelands, common lands, alleyways, and terraced back yards. All lost to urbanisation, unsafe roads and to the fear of strangers. Play is the avenue to education for children, to prepare them for life, providing the training blocks for their futures. Whether through free expression or competitive activities, all forms of play are of equal value in this process. It is very important that all of children's play equipment should reflect their multi-cultural ethnic requirements. This is particularly more so if they happen to live in an inner city or multi racial community. The range and type of play equipment provided should be specifically geared to their age range and gender. It should include toys and equipment that specifically covers the areas which are most beneficial to their overall, individual and group play needs. Play has many functions: it gives children a chance to be together, with their peers an opportunity to share and build together with a chance to use their bodies, to build muscles, and to test new skills. But above all, play is a function of the imagination. A child's play is his or her way of dealing with the issues of his growth, of relieving tensions and exploring the world and a means of preparing for the future.

At the present time in 2020 there are over 80 adventure playgrounds in London alone.

Holland park adventure playground

"It comes down to this: I am not a leader, but a servant to the children."(Jack Lambert).

To work with children who were anxious and eager to play their games of pretence and fun,was for me, and still is an extraordinary adventure.

Ray Wills

SOURCES RESOURCES AND RECCOMMENDED READINGS

Towards a history of adventure playgrounds 1931–2000 Keith Cranwell

REVOLUTIONARY PLAY WORK AND REFLECTIVE
ANALYTICAL PRACTICE
- BOB HUGHES

TOWARDS A SAFER ADVENTURE PLAYGROUND
-BILL MCCULLOUGH AND FRANK KING

ADVENTURE PLAYGROUNDS By ARVID BENGTSSON
-CROSBY LOCKWOOD 1972

ADVENTURE PLAYGROUNDS By JACK LAMBERT
- PENGUINS 1977

SOMETHING EXTRAORDINARY By H.S PAT TURNER
-MICHAEL JOSEPH 1961

PLAY LEADERSHIP -N.P.F.A

ADVENTURE PLAYGROUNDS - N.P.F.A.

MEMOIRS OF AN UNEDUCATED LADY
LADY MARJORIE ALLEN OF HURTWOOD and MARY
NICHOLSON

ALLEN AND NICHOLSON
-THAMES AND HUDSON 1975

PLANNING FOR PLAY By
LADY MARJORIE ALLEN

GROUNDS FOR PLAY By JOE BENJAMIN
- LIVERPOOL COUNCIL OF SOCIAL SERVICES

IN SEARCH OF ADVENTURE
By JOE BENJAMIN

A study of the junk playground, Nuffield Foundation, 1961

ADVENTURE PLAYGROUNDS A BRIEF HISTORY -TONY
CHILTON

FAIR PLAY FOR CHUILDREN -2013

ASPECTS OF PLAY WORK
By BOB HUGHES and FRASER BROWN

Printed in Great Britain
by Amazon